TRIAGE

The art of business turnarounds

Stephen Barnes

First published in 2024 by Stephen Barnes

A catalogue entry for this book is available from the National Library of Australia.

ISBN: 978-1-923007-43-7

Printed in Australia by Pegasus
Book production and text design by Publish Central
Cover design by Julia Kuris

The paper this book is printed on is environmentally friendly.

Disclaimer: Neither the publisher nor the author is engaged in rendering professional advice or services to the reader. The ideas, suggestions, legal interpretations, and procedures provided in this book are not intended as a substitute for seeking professional guidance. Making adjustments to a financial strategy or plan should only be undertaken after consulting with a professional. Neither the publisher nor the author makes any guarantee or shall be held liable or responsible for any loss or damage allegedly arising from any suggestion or information contained in this book.

Contents

Part IV: Formal insolvency options 181

Foreword

In the ever-changing world of business, one undeniable truth stands out: constant change and disruption have become the new norm. All businesses, regardless of their size or sector, are grappling with the impact of digitisation and technological transformation.

Recent events have significantly shaped the global business landscape, especially in the realm of corporate restructuring. Jurisdictions worldwide are in a continual scramble to upgrade insolvency legislation, aiming to rescue financially distressed yet otherwise viable businesses. In the US, the UK, Europe, India, and Asia, academics and practitioners are exploring innovative approaches to enhance the corporate terrain. They seek to use legislative reform, 'preventative restructuring', and pre-insolvency frameworks to improve asset protection and limited liability for entrepreneurs.

Commonly mentioned is the US Chapter 11 and the shift from 'creditor-in-possession' to 'debtor-in-possession' regimes. The latter allows the director to remain in control of the business and take responsibility for its survival. While Commonwealth jurisdictions have historically favoured the former, the majority of jurisdictions have sought to improve business outcomes through continual adjustments, monitoring and guidance. Unfortunately, Australia seems to have lagged behind in this regard. As the global economy faces challenges, Australia's leading academics emphasise the importance and urgency of legislative change. Although many restructuring regimes still need improvement, Australia seems to have finally joined the race after acknowledging that rescuing viable businesses leads to better outcomes for businesses, creditors, employees, and ultimately the economy.

In 2017, Australia took its first step towards this concept with the introduction of the 'safe harbour for directors' legislation. The new section 588GA provides eligible directors with protection from personal liability for insolvent trading if a restructuring and turnaround plan is prepared (with the Hon. Kelly O'Dwyer MP clarifying that 'hope is not a strategy.'). In January 2021, the government introduced a simplified debt restructuring process for eligible small businesses. This process, subject to certain thresholds, allows directors to stay in control of their business and continue trading while proposing a debt compromise to creditors. Unfortunately, there remains issues surrounding small businesses' ability to access these recent legislative turnaround and restructuring initiatives.

The book *Triage: The art of business turnarounds* couldn't have come at a more opportune time. On 12 July, 2023, the Parliamentary Joint Committee announced the results of an eight-month Corporate Insolvency Inquiry review after receiving 78 submissions from a diverse range of the community. Identifying the corporate insolvency system as too complex, hard to access, and unnecessarily costly, the committee made 28 recommendations. These herald the long-awaited 'root and branch' review of insolvency, the most significant event in Australian insolvency law history since the Harmer Report in 1988. Many of these recommendations can be attributed to the expert analysis and insight of a few insolvency law academics and several pioneering Business Restructuring and Turnaround Practitioners.

In the business realm, another truth often overlooked emerges – one that has eluded directors, business advisors, and the Australian Government: the root causes of struggling businesses are frequently hiding in plain sight. Often attributed to the Dutch philosopher Desiderius Erasmus and frequently quoted in the business community is the term 'prevention is better than cure'. Stephen Barnes fearlessly confronts the truth about business turnaround, urging a keen eye and the courage to address fundamental components beyond the legal entity or corporate vessel.

Triage: The art of business turnarounds logically begins with diagnosing the business, challenging conventional notions using clear analogies to redefine what it takes to turn a business around. In this era of contemporary business turnaround, Stephen Barnes dissects the essence of running a business, demonstrating that principles remain steadfast amid changing circumstances.

The journey unfolds in four phases, correcting Australasia's approach to business turnaround. *Triage: The art of business turnarounds*, deferring formal insolvency options until the final phase, meticulously unveils the priorities in a complex turnaround. Business triage, inspired by the medical field, is portrayed as an art – a roadmap using Analysis, Emergency, and Crisis Stabilisation phases to divert a business from collapse.

Stephen Barnes dissects business operations, revealing overlooked fundamentals that underpin success. The revelation emerges that every business, irrespective of legal structure, shares common vulnerabilities and transformation potential. 'Triage as an art' is comprehensively featured, highlighting the skillsets required for a business revival.

Returning to more 'heavy-handed' tools, Stephen Barnes guides readers to the latest formal insolvency options in Australia and

New Zealand, providing invaluable insights for businesses on the brink of financial crisis. *Triage: The art of business turnarounds* promises a transformative experience, challenging reflection on personal and managerial effectiveness.

Triage: The art of business turnarounds is more than a guide; it is a mirror reflecting Stephen Barnes's experience and passion for saving businesses. It demands introspection and inspires action, serving as a clarion call for directors and advisors to adopt triage as an art. The aim is to confront business core issues and root causes for distress, empowering directors and business owners to emerge stronger, more resilient, and better equipped for future challenges, steering clear of expensive and value-destroying formal insolvency options.

Eddie Griffith
Chair
Association for Business Restructuring and Turnaround

Preface

'No matter how far down the wrong road you've gone you can always turn around.'

Turkish proverb

Business is hard! I have never heard anyone say it's easy, yet each year thousands of brave people start a business. At almost the same rate each year thousands of businesses fail, get into financial distress and/or cease operating. However, it is the 'dash' that matters.[1] In between starting and ceasing, there is a journey. The type of business, the structure of the business, the location, products, industry and people are different from one business to the next, but the business lifecycle is invariably the same: startup, growth, maturity, decline, cease operating.

This book is written for businesses in the decline phase, and while focused on business turnarounds and restructuring, it's equally applicable to everyday management. Just like a car battery that is

---

1   *The Dash* by Linda Ellis is a contemplative poem where 'the dash' represents our life. The dash that Linda Ellis refers to is the one that comes between the year of our birth and the year of our death. The dash is the representation of life itself.

going flat, if we keep the engine running the alternator will recharge the battery and it is likely the car will start next time. Don't keep the engine running and the battery will go completely flat and it will be impossible to start the car. Many businesses in the start of decline could benefit from a dose of some preventative turnaround medicine too. They need to keep the engine running. A business that has been recently acquired often needs some remedial medicine too.

Turnaround opportunities exist everywhere in a business – be it in a retail store, manufacturing, product lines and offerings, or looking at divisions and subsidiaries. You are always competing in business, and you must earn that right to compete every day – day after day. The basics of a turnaround are the same principles that help every business compete and survive, so this book may be useful in that context too.

I do want to congratulate you for picking up this book and starting on your business turnaround and restructuring journey. This very act of picking up and reading this book has given you and your business a far better chance of not ceasing, not failing, and you may even prosper and exceed your expectations.

I do not know of any business owner who starts a business without the intention and desire to make it a success. Success is an individual and personal thing – success might be enough to earn a living to support a lifestyle. Success might be to own a multinational conglomerate. Success might be the smile on the face of the person that bought your product or service.

Failure too is an individual and personal thing. If your business fails you may feel you have failed your family, your customers or clients, your creditors, your staff and your investors. But to me it is not you that has failed, it is your business that has failed. You as an individual are just a part of that business.

The three types of business failure

There are three types of business failure:

1. **The startup that never starts:** this may be due to the market not existing, being undercapitalised to grow or to endure a shock, being unable to survive the competitive forces of bigger firms catching up and entering the market, or the person running the business is not a businessperson.

2. **The catastrophic failure:** the business suffers a major event such as a flood, fire, cyber-attack, fraud, lawsuit or change in regulations.

3. **Normal business failure:** the incremental failure over time.

This book is written predominately about normal business failure, though the advice can be applied to startup and catastrophic business failures, or even businesses that are performing quite well.

Normal business failure follows the trajectory in the diagram below. This book covers the periods from step 2 to step 6 – under-performance to stabilisation.

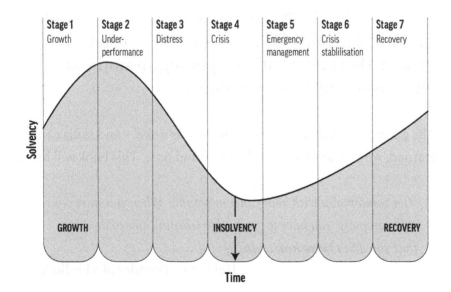

In my decades working in the business turnaround field, I have heard all sorts of 'reasons' a business has failed. Most are what I would describe as excuses or symptoms rather than reasons. These are usually outwardly focused; for example, global recession, the retail market is in the doldrums, the main customer has gone belly up, the currency exchange rate has gone up (or down), or the cost of a key input has gone up. All things that a business owner has no, or little, control over.

But ships don't sink because of water around them. Ships sink because of water that gets in them. Don't let what's happening around you get inside and bring you down.

There are, in my opinion, three valid reasons for a business to be ailing. Your business is not running so well, or could run better, due to one or more of the following:

- A lack of business skills in the business.
- A lack of attention to applying business skills within the business.
- You are spending the majority of time working *in* the business rather than *on* the business.

> ❛ But ships don't sink because of water around them. Ships sink because of water that gets in them. Don't let what's happening around you get inside and bring you down.

The good news is that running a business is a skill – and skills can be learned. All you need is some devotion and time. This book will help.

'Get comfortable with being uncomfortable. When you start your own company, you have to get used to learning how to do things that you don't know how to do.'

Heidi Zak, Founder of Thirdlove

Running a business often becomes an 'addiction'. The way to satisfy an addiction is to get *more*. Alcoholics need another drink, drug addicts need more drugs, and business owners need to work harder and longer. But as with all addicts, this approach may satisfy their short-term need but it is not good for them in the long term. To treat an addict, you must subscribe to a form of relief. Smokers use nicotine patches and heroin addicts use methadone.

Overcoming an addiction isn't a simple process. In fact, it may be more accurate to think of it like a journey in which you venture through uncharted territories before finally reaching your destination.

The book *Changing for Good* breaks the addiction recovery process into six stages, which are sometimes referred to as the Transtheoretical Model.[2] The stages are:

1. pre-contemplation
2. contemplation
3. preparation
4. action
5. maintenance
6. termination.

Each stage corresponds to a particular phase in an individual's journey from active addiction to lasting sobriety. Moreover, these six stages essentially decipher the rehabilitation process, making it easier to understand by reducing the long road to recovery into a series of distinct checkpoints. Of course, understanding the importance of this model requires a closer look at each of these six stages.

With a turnaround process, the same stages are applicable, and it starts with the pre-contemplation phase. In reading this book you are at this stage. Use this book as a tool, but for the turnaround to succeed you must have the desire and willingness to make changes

---

2 Norcross, Prochaska, & DiClemente, 1994.

and, like an addict, follow through the stages and enact the changes. Reading the book alone will not be enough. It is a reference guide that addresses the reasons your business is in decline, distress or failing, and a practical guide to how to turn your business around. The information you need is here, but you must act on it.

Most people don't read business books from cover to cover, and I expect this book will be no different. I first discuss what the turnaround process and business triage is and the causes of corporate decline. Parts II to III discuss the triage steps in a turnaround and restructure process. Finally, there is a brief overview of formal insolvency options in Australia and New Zealand.

Your business may have a particular area that needs some focus, and you can move directly to that part of the book. The book looks great in a bookcase, but I'd rather you have a battered, well-read copy handy. Come back and go over a chapter or a concept again just like you would keep referring to a manual when fixing an appliance. Have a physical copy of the book on your desk to refer to so when you are watching TV or are away from the office and an idea or question pops up you have easy access to the book.

While the book discusses business turnaround and transformation, and looks at the business as a whole, many of the ideas and concepts can also be utilised down to a project level. My team and I have worked on turning around major projects and utilised many of the same concepts in this book to do so.

Introduction

In many respects, businesses are like people. People are similar and yet unique at the same time. They may be located in different countries, in cities or in regional areas. They may be newborn, young, mature, or nearing end of life. They may be good at some things and not so good at others. They will have different interests, and some are introverts while others are extroverts. Some will belong to big families, and some will be alone.

Like people, businesses sometimes get sick. Sickness may occur over a period or be sudden and traumatic. When people are at a serious stage of illness, they often end up at the hospital emergency department.

The first person they see is a triage nurse.

What is triage?

Triage comes from the French verb *trier*, which means the sorting of patients according to the urgency of their need for care.[3] Triage is the process of determining the priority of each patient's treatment

---

3   Merriam-Webster Online Dictionary, 2020.

by the severity of their condition or likelihood of recovery with and without treatment. This allocates patient treatment efficiently when resources are insufficient for all to be attended to immediately, influencing the order and priority of emergency treatment. The triage nurse will assign a different priority and resources to a person presenting with a fractured finger compared to a person presenting with a stroke.

Medical triage was 'invented' as a strategy in the Napoleonic Wars by Dominique Jean Larrey. He was a surgeon who treated the wounded from the battlefield according to the severity of injuries and the urgency of care, with no regard for their rank or what side they were fighting on. Triage was then used in World War I by French doctors – hence the origin of the name of the strategy. The people responsible for removing the injured from the battlefield would classify the victims into:

- Those who are likely to live, regardless of what care they receive.
- Those who are unlikely to live, regardless of what care they receive.
- Those for whom immediate care may make a positive difference in outcome.

The same concept and strategy are still used today, though we are now more scientific in the assessment, with models such as S.T.A.R.T. (simple triage and rapid treatment), and G.C.S. (Glasgow Coma Scale), and triage scales – Black/Expectant, Red/Immediate, Yellow/Observation, Green/Wait, White/Dismiss – or in Australian and New Zealand a time scale from one to five with standard times in which a patient should be seen.

There is also an ethical element to triage as one person's rights and treatment is weighed up against another person's and the resources of the hospital or emergency worker. This complicates the decision-making process and adds stress to the situation for the triage responder, and indeed the patient and their families. Especially in disaster situations, a utilitarian approach is used: the triage decisions maximise the outcomes and the resources used to produce benefits for the most people possible.

Once a patient has been triaged, a plan is developed for their treatment. This may include different operations, the timing and sequencing of treatments, medications, and rehabilitation strategies. Often various operations and treatments will happen simultaneously. As treatment is undertaken other issues and problems might surface, and the treatment plan needs to be modified. Priorities might also change during the treatment. Sometimes plan A does not lead to the desired or expected outcome so the doctors need to pivot to plan B. At all stages, a clear vision is essential and needs to be understood by all stakeholders. Often when the patient leaves the hospital they are not fully recovered and treatment may continue for weeks, months or even years.

What is business triage?

In a business context, triage is about assessing the situation and assigning levels of priorities to people and tasks to determine the most effective order in which to deal with them to achieve the desired outcome.[4] It is crisis management and requires triage of the processes, people and tasks, prioritising competing resources – time, money, people – in a deteriorating situation that requires swift action.

Like in the medical triage classification, in business the classifications would be:

- Issues unlikely to cause further problems, regardless of the actions taken.

---

4 Bizshifts-Trends, 2018.

- Issues likely to cause further problems, regardless of the actions taken.
- Issues in which immediate action might make a positive difference in outcome.

Triage in a business sense is also utilitarian in that it is assessing what resources are available and determining how those resources can be utilised to serve the goal of the best outcome for the overall business and all stakeholders. Business triage in a turnaround or transformation situation is also not static – it is a continuous process that requires constantly assessing all available resources minute by minute, hour by hour, and day by day. It needs to be flexible enough to pivot during fluid situations.

In most businesses, triage is occurring subconsciously. It may be on a small problem or just something that is par for the course of daily operations. Think of a café when a customer asks for a chai coffee. If it is not on the menu, you enter into a triage situation. The server assesses the situation and the customer and classifies the situation as either unlikely to cause a problem if they just reply no they do not serve chai coffee, or assesses the situation and determines that regardless of their reply, the customer has moved on and ordered something else. Or they assess the situation and determine that regardless of whether they offer an alternative, the customer would complain and be dissatisfied.

❛ 'In a business context, triage is about assessing the situation and assigning levels of priorities to people and tasks to determine the most effective order in which to deal with them to achieve the desired outcome.'

One of the problems though in subconscious triage is that decisions are more likely to be emotional rather than logical. They are automatic reactions. Often a business in decline has been making many micro triage decisions, however it is all too easy to panic and make knee-jerk decisions. In a business turnaround or transformation context these knee-jerk reactions and subconscious triage have usually led to the situation they find themselves in. What they should be doing is stepping back and viewing the big picture – standing on the balcony looking at the dance floor. Then the triage decisions change from emotional and reactive to logical, rational and strategic.

There is a 19th century fable of the 'boiled frog'. Once a frog jumped in a pot of water that had been put on a stove. As the water in the pot heated up the frog remained in the water, and as frogs do, adjusted its body temperature to the temperature of the water. But as the water reached boiling point the frog was unable to keep up adjusting its body temperature and got boiled alive.

If, however, you had put the frog in a pot of boiling water it would have jumped straight out again. Often it takes a shock to create the necessary action.

The moral of the story is the frog could not make it due to its own inability to decide when it had to jump out. We all need to adjust according to a situation, but there are times when we need to face the situation and take the appropriate action when we have the strength to do so, before it is too late. Walk out before you need to jump. Also don't wait until the pot has boiled, or the business problems have escalated, before you take the necessary action.[5]

---

5 Science tells us that this story is false, at least for frogs. But might it apply to humans? Scientists recently found evidence that humans may in fact be strikingly similar to the fabled boiling frog (Moore & Obradovich, 2019).

What is a business turnaround?

A business turnaround is everyday management, but on steroids. It is the process of taking a company in serious decline or distress that will fail in the foreseeable future if corrective action is not undertaken on a journey to achieve a better outcome. It is taking traditional management and applying it in an unusual situation: the business is in trouble.

'Turnaround management is a process dedicated to corporate renewal. It uses analysis and planning to save troubled companies and return them to solvency, and to identify the reasons for failing performance in the market, and rectify them.'[6]

It is often thought that business turnaround is short-term focused and only looks at cost reductions. It is, however, much broader and more holistic, focusing on both operational and strategic issues simultaneously. It is both short- and long-term focused. It is both soft and hard in its approach.

The objectives of a business turnaround are:[7]

- Take control and manage the immediate crisis.
- Rebuild stakeholder support.
- Fix the business.
- Resolve future funding.

> ❛ 'Turnaround management is a process dedicated to corporate renewal. It uses analysis and planning to save troubled companies and return them to solvency, and to identify the reasons for failing performance in the market, and rectify them.'

---

6 Wikipedia.
7 Slatter & Lovett, 1999.

The scope of the turnaround typically follows four phases:

- **Analysis phase:** This is where a diagnostic review is performed and turnaround options are evaluated.

- **Emergency phase:** The turnaround team is established and a plan developed, and the immediate crisis actions are undertaken. There is usually a heavy focus on liquidity management, operational factors, cost control and stabilising sales.

- **Crisis Stabilisation phase:** This phase looks at areas that will strengthen the business going forward. This might be revisiting standard operating procedures or looking at IT systems and processes. It may also look at product and markets, and making decisions about what changes are required for ongoing and long-term viability.

- **Growth and Renewal phase:** Once the business balance sheet has improved, the business can begin to grow again, either organically or via merger or acquisition, or both.

The 'art' of a turnaround is like tending a sick tree. You have to balance fixing the tree's immediate problems with making it grow better in the future. It's a bit like pruning the tree. When the tree's roots can't support it, you need to find and cut off the dead or dying branches. This way, the healthy parts can get the food they need. It's also tough to trim back new shoots and branches that are taking too much from the tree.

Underlying and throughout these four phases, the turnaround specialist also undertakes stakeholder management and project management.

In this book only the issues and processes in the first three phases will be discussed. The first three phases are not linear; the issues and tasks overlap, and action occurs to some degree simultaneously. Having addressed the first three phases, the fourth phase has a good foundation. I have seen too many businesses getting themselves into distress by focusing on growth, and too many turnarounds that stall or fail when the focus reverts too quickly to the growth phase.

The turnaround process end to end is not quick and would typically take between 1½ and 2 years. The more engaged boards and owners are in the turnaround the more they can do, usually leading to a better outcome in a shorter amount of time. It may also mean they would only need a turnaround specialist for the Analysis and Emergency phases and not the entire turnaround.

What is a turnaround specialist?

Turnaround specialists are not Chief Financial Officers (CFOs) and accountants, and they are not lawyers, salespeople or marketing experts. They are not hatchet people only interested in cutting costs and staff, as portrayed in some films and media. They may, however, have qualifications and expertise in some of these areas. My definition of a turnaround specialist is a 'polymathic crisis manager'.

Polymaths are individuals whose knowledge spans a significant number of subjects, and who are known to draw on complex bodies of knowledge to solve specific problems. Crisis managers are responsible for planning and implementing the response to a major threat to a business.

Turnaround specialists come to a business with complete objectivity, and with the ability to quickly analyse the situation and determine solutions and actions that those in or close to the business may not be able to see. They can also make the critical and timely decisions that need to be made free of the emotional bias of the shareholders, directors and management. Turnaround specialists also have a unique management style and range of behavioural skills. They like being shoulder deep in the operations, and like intense situations. They have to work with often inaccurate and incomplete data and use their intuition to make decisions. They build credibility by delivering on what they say they will do and building trust. Being a CFO or a corporate banker does not translate into being a turnaround specialist. It is the other skills and knowledge, and the ability to apply them, that really make a turnaround specialist.

There are two 'truths' about all businesses that may seem contradictory but are complementary:

- **All businesses are the same.** All businesses buy and sell goods and services, must manage staff, production, workflow, have bills to pay and receivables to collect, and tax returns to submit. They are all the same.
- **All businesses are different.** Every business has different people, processes, culture. They have a different way of doing things, and their own 'secret sauce'. They are all different.

It doesn't necessarily matter if a turnaround consultant does not come from the same industry as yours. They will understand that all businesses are the same and all businesses are different. In fact, getting a turnaround consultant who only works in the one industry may add to a 'groupthink' problem. You want your turnaround consultant to be an objective observer and an active participant.

There are also some things you should not expect from a turnaround specialist. They are not miracle workers – they will do their best with what they have. Also, their success at implementing a turnaround is reliant on the support of the board and management team, who need to own the turnaround and commit to the actions required. Turnaround specialists usually do not work alone but require a team, both internally and externally, working on the turnaround for it to be successful.

Business restructuring in Australia and New Zealand has been predominately creditor-centric. In other words, it is focused more towards preserving investments by creditors – primarily suppliers, banks and the Tax Office. The creditors ultimately decide the fate of the company, and the formal insolvency practitioners work for the best outcome of the creditors alone. In the United States and Europe a debtor-centric model is predominant, whereby actions taken are for the best interests of the company and all its stakeholders (including creditors). Control of the process remains in the hands of the directors.

In September 2017 what are known as the Safe Harbour provisions of the Corporations Act were introduced to allow for some scope to use a debtor-centric process. While the Safe Harbour provisions do not have the same legal protections for company directors, they do remain in control of the business and act in the best interests of the business and not the best interests of the creditors. Unfortunately, this also saw a rise in many management consultants (and even insolvency practitioners) claiming turnaround expertise.

Out of an Australian Government Productivity Commission report in December 2000 it was determined that the creditor-centric model was stifling entrepreneurship and businesses were entering insolvency processes out of fear of directors' personal liability.

In February 2021, and in response to the COVID pandemic, the Australian Government introduced a middle-ground process call Small Business Restructuring. A registered Small Business Restructuring Practitioner (SBRP) is appointed by the directors to help them look at their company debts and negotiate an easier payback plan. The SBRP deals with creditors to agree on delayed payments and reduced payments or debt. The process is short – 20 days – and if successful the SBRP oversees the dividend process while directors continue to manage their day-to-day business.

I agree with the December 2000 Productivity Commission report – the current insolvency processes in Australia do not help businesses succeed. Most small businesses that enter a formal insolvency option do not survive. Formal insolvency processes are usually employed at a stage when options are few and the process has become about preserving creditor value, rather than helping the business and ensuring all stakeholders benefit.

This book is ultimately about helping businesses in crisis survive. It will be taking a debtor-centric approach. When looking at a debtor-centric turnaround or restructure, consider the following points from an *American Bankruptcy Institute Journal* article:[8]

- Turnaround consulting is a complex operational exercise in providing experienced leadership to quickly and drastically reshape the business for improved performance. It requires persuading highly reluctant managers, owners and investors to execute painful changes they have constantly avoided, usually over a long period of time. It also requires the impatient creditors to give a window of time for change to occur.

- Turnaround professionals usually also need restructuring skills. Often, they are engaged so late that inadequate time remains to execute a turnaround alone, and/or lender fatigue has set in so heavily that patience has been exhausted.

- Turnaround consultants provide leadership under trying conditions and successful turnaround consultants are nearly always proven, experienced business leaders, generally not consultants or advisors by background.

Skilled turnaround consultants first take a careful assessment of the 'degree of distress'. This book is called *Triage* as the turnaround process is analogous to an emergency room doctor or nurse assessing an incoming patient. Their subsequent actions depend greatly

---

8   Morris, 2004.

on the assessment of the patient and dictates whether one wields a scalpel, knife or hatchet – and whether there is time for analysis, contemplation and buy-in versus a requirement for immediate, often draconian, action.

Why you need to act early

If I did a poll of past clients, almost without exception they would say they refused to acknowledge the signs of business crisis to avoid admitting mistakes. They refused to acknowledge the signs of crisis to themselves, and if they cannot admit this to themselves, they will not admit it to anyone else. Unfortunately, not recognising there's a problem is a surefire path to liquidation.

As soon as there is even the slightest indication of a crisis, you need to concede and act quickly and decisively. Jumping on the problem straight away not only boosts your chances of survival, it also demonstrates strong leadership – a critical trait to win and keep stakeholder confidence.

❝ 'If I did a poll of past clients, almost without exception they would say they refused to acknowledge the signs of business crisis to avoid admitting mistakes.'

In Ernest Hemingway's book *The Sun Also Rises*, the character Mike is asked how he went bankrupt. 'Two ways,' he answers. 'Gradually, then suddenly.' A client, Andy, rang me one day and said, 'I've been running a business for eight years, it's profitable, it has grown, but I don't have any money.' Six weeks later he filed a debtor petition for bankruptcy. His business had gradually gone bankrupt over eight years – and then it did. His debts were so large, and his wait to seek help so delayed, that the best course of action was to file for bankruptcy.[9] Every pre-insolvency, turnaround or insolvency advisor's number one wish for any potential client is to **seek help early**. The earlier you get help, just like if you need medical attention, the greater the likelihood of a good outcome.

How to use this book

While this book is for businesses in distress or crisis, it can be used by any existing business up to the stage they have to enter a formal insolvency process – voluntary administration, small business restructuring, liquidation or receivership. Your business may not yet be in crisis but could operate better, and the Analysis or the Crisis Stabilisation sections may just be enough for you. Or your business may be in crisis and nearly in liquidation – go straight to the Emergency section. Your business may have been through tough times, made some changes and be ready to stabilise and move forward – go to the strategic change section. But this is ultimately a thought-provoking book that asks the reader to critically look at their business and how to manage it successfully. I therefore recommend reading it completely, and then re-read it a few days later after absorbing the content in relation to your business and circumstances. Don't wait weeks, months or years between reading and re-reading the book, and take action – a lack of action will not improve your situation, and your options diminish over time.

---

9   My business, Byronvale Advisors, did come up with a solution that turned the business around with Andy as a key person, and then returned the business to Andy profitable, sustainable and growing.

Part I

ANALYSIS PHASE

'm going to give away a big secret – I'm analysing you and your business from the very first interaction I have with you. The first contact page submission, the first email, the first phone call or meeting, and the first time I come to your premises. Subconsciously business owners, directors and management give me signs, tell me about symptoms and causes, and have predictors as to the state their business is in, their aptitude, attitude and energy to complete a successful restructure or turnaround.

There are numerous predictors, signs, causes and symptoms that give information as to what the problems are (there are always numerous problems), and if it is possible to turn the business around or restructure it.

Let's take a look at some of these.

Chapter 1

Predictors of problems

There are three categories of financial distress predictors:

- empirical models
- 'zombies'
- observations.

Empirical models

Empirical business failure models can be grouped broadly into quantitative and qualitative models. Quantitative models look at published financial information, and therefore are only useful for large, publicly listed businesses. Qualitative models are based on assessments of internal factors and characteristics. Both try to provide a measure that ranks the analysed business beside known failed businesses.

Quantitative models

One of the better known corporate failure prediction models is the Z-Altman score. The Z-Altman score – developed by Edward Altman – uses linear discriminant analysis with five financial ratios to predict the likelihood of corporate failure in the next two years.

I ran the Z-Altman score on Virgin Australia – a company that the directors placed into voluntary administration shortly after the COVID-19 pandemic began in Australia. Looking at the publicly available information as at June 2019, the Z-Altman result strongly indicated corporate failure nine months before the start of the pandemic. The pandemic was more the final nail in the coffin and not the cause of the company failure, as Virgin Australia was already in a dire position.

The H-score (or health score, not to be confused with the medical H-score that estimates the risk of reactive hemophagocytic syndrome) also looks at a range of financial ratios, but compares the same ratios to a set of failed businesses and looks to see how close they are as a predictor of business failure.

There is also Robert C. Merton's 1974 Distance to Default model, which was later modified by Fischer Black and Myron Scholes to develop their Nobel Prize–winning Black-Scholes pricing model for options.

And there are various other models used by different businesses under different circumstances.

Qualitative models

The Argenti A-score looks at the health of a business by comparing some key non-financial information to that of failed businesses. Argenti suggests that business failure follows a predictable sequence: defects (both management and accounting), mistakes made (for example, high debt, overtrading or a massive project), and symptoms of failure (financial signs, creative accounting, non-financial signs and terminal signs). The closer your business is to the failed business the greater the predictor of failure.

Have a go at the Argenti score yourself by completing the test below. Cross out the statements that *do not* apply to your business, and then add up the total score for the remaining statements.

Management	• The business is run by an autocrat.	8
	• The chief executive and chairperson are the same individual.	4
	• The other directors are non-existent, passive or non-contributing.	2
	• Your business lacks directors with all-round skills.	2
	• There is a specific lack of a strong finance director.	2
	• Your business lacks management depth below board level.	1
Accounting controls	• There is no budgetary control, budgets or variance reports.	3
	• There are no up-to-date cashflow plans and no or poor knowledge of borrowing requirements.	3
	• Your business has no costing system so that the costs and contribution of each product are unknown.	3
Adaptability	• There are poor responses to changes in the business environment, old-fashioned products, obsolete factory, old directors and out-of-date marketing.	15
Mistakes and risks	• High leverage or levels of borrowing.	15
	• Overtrading, with company expanding faster than its funding, and capital base is too small or unbalanced for the size and type of company.	15
	• Big project gone wrong or exposed or at risk of collapse if a big project goes wrong.	15

Warning signs	• Signs of financial difficulty, such as poor accounting ratios or poor Z-Altman score.	4
	• Creative accounting to disguise financial difficulties.	4
	• Non-financial signs of difficulty, such as untidy offices, frozen salaries, high staff turnover, CEO is 'ill' rumours.	3
	• Terminal signs, such as bank reduces overdraft facility or suppliers go COD.	1
Total possible score		**100**

Now that you have your A-score, use the table below to take appropriate action.

Score	Result
Less than 10	Things are pretty good and there is no cause for alarm.
10–25	Some cause for concern. Look at the areas highlighted by the test and take action to address them.
Over 25	Serious concern – get help now (preferably from an experienced turnaround advisor).

Scorecard tests

Both quantitative and qualitative models, however, are only useful for larger businesses with established financial reporting and financial statements. Usually small businesses, and especially the ones in crisis, do not have the financial information required for these models to be useful.

For smaller businesses a 'scorecard test' might be a good predictor. The scorecard poses a number of non-financial questions on holistic areas of the business, such as management, attitude to change, accounting management, risk management, controls and signs (see below). Each question is weighted, and the sum totals 100. Your total for your business indicates the level of concern for its survival.

Zombies

'Zombie companies' – also known as 'zombie firms' or the 'living dead' – is a term used for businesses unable to stand on their own. They either need one or a series of bailouts or are kept afloat by lenient creditors and financiers and low interest rates. Often, they are only one event away from becoming insolvent.

The term 'zombie company' originated in Japan to describe companies that were only generating enough cash to pay interest on their debts. After the collapse of the Japanese asset price bubble in late 1991, Japanese banks continued to support weak or failing firms instead of letting them go bankrupt. This contributed to what is known as the 'lost decade', a period of economic stagnation in Japan.

In 2008, during the Global Financial Crisis, the term regained popularity and was used to describe companies that were bailed out by the U.S. Troubled Asset Relief Program (TARP).

The COVID-19 pandemic has accentuated zombie company visibility, but the reality is that the re-emergence of zombie companies has been occurring for several years. Tony Kaye, editor of the *Eureka Report*, in November 2018 (long before the pandemic) claimed that one in five ASX[10] companies, and 12% of all companies globally, were classified as zombies, though it was much smaller percentage wise in market value. The main industries where zombies were found were capital-intensive industries such as energy and

---

10 Australian Securities Exchange.

mining, and companies with negative current operational cashflows such as fast-growth IT companies.

For zombies to emerge there first needs to be the 'right' environment. One common feature is low interest rates. Japan in the 'lost decade' had near zero interest rates. Low interest rates do two things: firstly, they take debt repayment pressure off companies. If interest rates were to rise, their interest coverage would worsen. Rising interest rates would also make it more difficult for these companies to roll over debt obligations.

Secondly, low interest rates put banks in a catch-22 situation with zombie companies. Morningstar equity analyst Gareth James said in an article, 'Lenders want companies to survive and pay back their loans. If you're a lender sending a company into bankruptcy, you're cutting your nose to spite your face. Lenders' first option would be to try and work it through. Capitalise the interest and give the company a holiday or renegotiate the terms.'[11] With the Banking Royal Commission and COVID-19 pandemic, Australasian banks have been reluctant to send companies into administration. Banks implemented deferral programs and were actively working with customers to keep them afloat. The 'Big 4' banks also ramped up their workout teams and made large provisions for bad loans, and these provisions are likely to increase. Post-pandemic, banks saw businesses (and individuals) increase their savings and have stronger balance sheets. However, with rampant inflation, labour shortages and supply chain shortages, these strong balance sheets rapidly dissipated and the number of businesses in distress increased, and the zombies were awakened.

Another zombie indicator is government bailouts. Throughout the world, governments have used various programs to support businesses through COVID-19. But again, we had also seen government

---

11 Rapaport, 2020.

bailouts prior to the pandemic. The car industry in Australia, which was supported time and again over a number of years, is one example. One by one Australian car manufacturers still closed.

Observations

Observations can help predict financial distress. When first assessing the situation of a business I take on various observer 'personas'. For each observer persona below, I have outlined some (not all) typical signs of a business in financial distress.

1. **'Man in the street':**
   - The business is subject to a takeover bid
   - Obsolete or hopeless products
   - A major disaster occurs
   - Loss of key personnel abruptly or embarrassingly
   - Public refinancing deals
   - Poor financial results
   - Serious profit warnings

   Consider Virgin Australia as an example. A few of these signs were evident from the position of the 'man in the street'.

2. **Informed person:**
   - Declining share price, profits, market share, liquidity, dividends, sales volume
   - Delays in publishing and qualification of accounts
   - New equity or debt raising to fund losses
   - Turnover of key staff
   - Public disagreements between directors and/or senior management

   The informed person might be a financial journalist or a 'mum and dad' investor. They take an interest in a particular business and the information about it.

3. **Analyst:**

   - Low morale
   - Loss of key customers
   - White elephant projects
   - Concealed board conflict
   - Loss of key personnel
   - Lack of strategy or ability to implement it
   - Breach of banking covenants
   - Discussion of financial restructuring plans
   - Share performance worse than sector average

4. **Suppliers and customers:**

   - Negotiations by suppliers with company bankers to support a restructuring plan
   - Factoring customer invoices[12]
   - Late payment of supplier invoices
   - Increased supplier disputes
   - Lengthening debtor and creditor days
   - Problems with new IT systems

5. **Investigating accountant:**

   - Poor working capital management
   - No sense of urgency
   - Creative accounting practices
   - Declining performance in the management accounts
   - Pending litigation matters
   - Lack of leadership

---

12 Factoring is a type of financing where the debt, and the responsibility for collecting that debt, is 'sold' to a finance company. The finance company pays the seller of the debt straight away, less commissions and interest.

6. **Employees:**

- Major management issues that can only be seen by the staff
- Emergency board meetings
- Management paralysis
- Finger pointing and bickering
- Acting in functional isolation
- Fear

So, as you can see there are many predictors of insolvency or impending insolvency.

Chapter 2

Insolvency signs, symptoms and causes

Common business failure signs

Business failure and frogs

Frogs – yes, frogs!

Several management writers have used frogs as a metaphor for management thinking, including Charles Handy in his book *The Age of Unreason* about the boiled frog and the theory we will not survive if we do not respond to the radical way the world is changing. Alistair Mant is a change management writer who also uses a frog as an analogy for change management resistance.

Frogs are used as a metaphor (according to Handy, Mant and other frog theorists) because:

- **Frogs are transformative.** They begin life in water swimming freely like a fish, and gradually grow and develop feet, and lungs instead of gills, and shed their tails, expand the size of their heads, and climb upon a rock and hop onto land.

- **Frogs are ancient creatures (approximately 190 million years old).** A frog reminds us that we all came from the same beginnings and share one common bond.
- **Frogs leap.** Frogs can leap up to 20 times their body length. So for great leaps forward, for transformational change and for sustainable existence – think frog.

Richardson et al classify reasons for business failure using the analogy of frogs, and categorise them by organisational size and frog-like characteristics, as shown in the table below.

Organisation/ leader type	Organisation size	
	Small	Big
Boiled frog	The hard-working, introverted family firm	The (s)lumbering giant
Drowned frog	The ambitious entrepreneur	The conglomerate kingmaker
Bullfrog	The small firm flash	The money-messing megalomaniac
Tadpole	The failed startup	The big project

Boiled frog

As discussed earlier there is a fable of the boiled frog. A frog jumped in a pot of water that had been put on a stove. As the water in the pot heated up the frog remained in the water, and as frogs do, adjusted its body temperature to the water. But as the water reached boiling point the frog was unable to keep up adjusting its body temperature and got boiled alive.

In a business failure context, the boiled frog theory focuses on failures of long-established businesses. These businesses have characteristics of introversion and inertia in the face of business environment change. Their problems build up slowly, the business owners and management are busy looking after the day-to-day and the business 'drifts' towards unavoidable crisis – just like the frog starting in cool water and failing to recognise the heat increasing until it is too late.

> ❝ Strategic drift is the business's failure to recognise and respond to changes within its business environment.

This drift is known as 'strategic drift'. Strategic drift is the business's failure to recognise and respond to changes within its business environment. While the business continues to make small steps forward these aren't sufficient to match the rapidly changing environment. The slow impact on the business can be hard to spot. Sometimes, the business's financial performance worsens, and the owners or management may not fully recognise the reasons behind this decline, which stem from the business drifting away from its external environment.

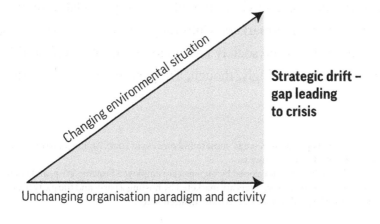

The slower you react, and the larger the gap between what you offer and what the customer demands, the harder it will be to transform.

A well-known example of boiled frog syndrome is Kodak.

Kodak had the people, technology and capital to pivot to digital and meet the demand for accessible photos from their customers. Kodak even invented the digital camera! However, they pursued film photography for another 10 years, neglecting the changing environment. Their failure was rooted in strategic drift: the gradual deterioration of competitive action that results in the failure of a business to acknowledge and respond to changes in the business environment.

A more recent, and ongoing, example of a boiled frog business is Tupperware.[13] Earl Tupper, a failed tree surgeon turned chemical engineer, invented the brightly coloured plastic containers in the 1940s. The company and products were literally a household name in the 1970s and the company was known for its 'party plan' system of selling its products.[14] However, this 'direct-to-consumer' model is no longer relevant in today's world. People are less likely to be at home as often, and have many other ways to catch up. People now have mobile phones, computers and better transport, so staying connected is easier and quicker. People also like to be able to access products immediately, with similar products more easily accessible, cheaper and more environmentally friendly available online and in shops and supermarkets. Culturally nowadays we are a disposable and just-in-time society and no longer have a cupboard full of containers. Interestingly, though, Tupperware did see a resurgence

---

13 Tupperware began a 'three-year' turnaround process in 2020. At time of writing it is still in the midst of this process.

14 Party plan selling was developed by Tupperware employee Brownie Wise, and is a form of direct selling where products are marketed by hosting a party and the party host presenting the products for sale to those in attendance.

during the COVID-19 pandemic as people were at home and did want to have supplies on hand.

There are a range of underlying causes of boiled frog business failure, suggested by a number of authors. Richardson et al summarised these thoughts as below. Consider the Tupperware and Kodak cases when reviewing these causes.

- **Complacency born of competitive success:** the business has a successful model or formula born out of an expansionist period when they enjoyed a competitive advantage. When the business environment changes there is no corresponding change to the business activity and there is a decline.

- **Top management blindness or they have their 'heads in the sand':** self-deception is a major cause of decline.

- **A hierarchy orientation:** aligning business goals with the company hierarchy rather than having market-oriented goals (of the business founders originally).

- **Cultural rigidity:** having a culture that managers are content to leave employees and resources where they are, even in the face of threats. The idea is to 'ride out the storm' by creating a stable and secure business that can – supposedly – survive any challenge.

- **Entrenchment of the status quo:** the 'we've always done it this way' attitude, and reluctance to do otherwise.

- **The search for consensus and compromise:** this is prevalent in large businesses where they have a meeting (or two or three) about everything (I called them ABMs – another bloody meeting). Responsibility is shared and diluted, which works against urgency and resolve.

- **The push for organisational growth rather than productive growth:** the business recruits new staff to drive growth, costs soar, and productivity does not change.

- **Benefits are awarded without equivalent increases in productivity:** real growth is rewarded by increased and improved benefits, however over time these improvements become the norm and there is no corresponding productivity boost.
- **Rising 'white-collar' costs:** white-collar roles are growing at a faster rate than blue-collar roles and technology is turning blue-collar jobs white, but with that, white-collar costs are increasing – and until recently (and maybe thanks to the pandemic) there has been less focus on productivity of white-collar roles (more looking at hours in the office than out, for example).
- **Low motivation of employees:** as employees have become more affluent, and societal values have evolved, traditional motivators may no longer be adequate.

Many businesses are suffering from boiled frog syndrome, and as such it is still an important concept to understand for taking stock of where your business might be now, and for addressing business failure.

Drowned frogs

Whereas boiled frog business failure is around management complacency, drowned frog business failure is more about ambition and hyperactivity of the leader.

What is a drowned frog leader?

The drowned frog leader is an overambitious, super-salesperson type who is so set on hyper-successful performance that they cease to believe in the existence of failure. Their personalities are recognisable. They are leaders of people, chatty, autocratic, restless and charismatic. Their ambition is so extreme that it could be described as almost pathological. They never accept advice; they 'know it all'. The analogy with drowned frogs according to Richardson et al is, 'a particular type of frog which is, itself, the creator of pond turbulence because of its insatiable need to be in many parts of the pond at more or less the same time, and because of its desire to create a position of "king of the pond" … Eventually, this often-worn-out frog drowns in a whirlpool of their own making.' They display the same characteristics in small and large businesses.

> ❛ The drowned frog leader is an overambitious, super-salesperson type who is so set on hyper-successful performance that they cease to believe in the existence of failure.

In a large business the drowned frog may represent a failed conglomerate kingmaker. They are expert 'contacts' people – a networker who forges relationships that can help them make growth happen. They usually have grand power aspirations and like to influence at a national, international or governmental level. An example is Robert Maxwell, the British media proprietor behind Pergamon and British Printing Corporation, member of parliament, suspected spy, fraudster, and father of the equally infamous Ghislaine Maxwell.[15]

Examples of drowned frogs may be Adam Neumann of WeWork infamy, and Travis Kalanick, the founder of Uber. Christopher Skase and Alan Bond would be Australian examples, and Ron Brierley a New Zealand example.

Drowned frog leaders usually have both 'saint' and 'sinner' roles during their careers – revered when they create success, and then they fall from grace in a dramatic fashion. The drowned frog leader exhibits an arrogance based on their belief that their early success can be reproduced, time after time, notwithstanding the new and different environment in which the latest success is sought.

---

15 Maxwell coincidentally did literally drown after apparently falling overboard from his yacht in the Atlantic Ocean. He was also used as inspiration for the villainous media baron Elliot Carver in the 1987 Bond movie *Tomorrow Never Dies*.

Drowned frog businesses have the characteristic of a swift trajectory to success and growth. The drowned frog leader is revered, and banks and financiers are easily predisposed to their exceptional level of persuasion (as with Adam Neumann and WeWork). Then the business garners public attention and there is an expectation for the media, the industry and the public of continued success and growth. By now normal governance standards have disappeared (if they existed in the first place) and the drowned frog leader perpetuates a 'one person show' approach to the management of the company. The turning point arrives with turnover still increasing but profits declining. The drowned frog leader reacts by taking growth, expansion and diversification to absurd levels in an attempt to keep the narrative alive for their backers and admirers. Creative accounting appears. Alarm starts to creep in from the financiers, and then an event occurs and collapse is rapid.

There are some causes and indicators for drowned frog business failure:

- **One-person rule:** drowned frog leaders are charismatic, opiniated, know-it-all super-salespeople. It is difficult to distinguish between a drowned frog leader and a super leader – but I would look at the management and governance structures surrounding them and their operations to make the distinction.

- **An ill-functioning board:** does the board work with the leader? If they work *for* the leader rather than *with* the leader this may indicate a drowned frog business. WeWork again is an example of this.

- **An unbalanced top team:** another feature of drowned frog businesses is a lack of a range of skills at the senior executive level, and the drowned frog leader surrounding themselves with subservient clones.

- **A weak finance function:** a lack of influential financial control in the business is common, with inadequate financial information systems and/or adverse messages they convey being disregarded by senior management.

Bullfrogs

Several years ago, I was working on an engagement in the industrial western suburbs of Melbourne. I made an observation to my wife one night that if you want to see European luxury cars, you would see more in those industrial western suburbs than you would in the 'affluent' eastern suburbs of Melbourne. Also, the top two industries for corporate insolvency in Australia are construction and transport – both dominant industries in the western suburbs. I bet if I had asked most of the Porsche- or Lamborghini-driving business owners how business was, they would say great, and then go to the pub to cry into a beer.

Bullfrogs are expensive show-offs who need to be seen with all the trappings of success, status and power. The problem with bullfrogs though is all the trappings they adorn themselves with create a situation where their lily-base (the supports) is not strong enough to bear the weight of the increasing adornments. The desire to be seen or perceived as a success means the lily eventually sinks to the bottom of the pond, taking the bullfrog and their all-important trappings with them.

> Bullfrogs are expensive show-offs who need to be seen with all the trappings of success, status and power.

Bullfrogs range from the 'small firm flash leader' to the 'money-messing megalomanic' – and they always spend money the business has not earned.

Most management theory would not recognise a small firm flash leader because management theory assumes:

- businesses have leaders who care about the business
- the business leader is the chief custodian of the business's prime objective – to survive – and the leader is that person most concerned about the business being economically productive
- the business leader is the architect of the strategy and overall process of the business
- the business leader is the 'conductor of the orchestra' of stakeholders.

However, a small firm flash leader is not an 'organisationalist', rather they are first and foremost about themselves. They follow these beliefs about businesses and business leaders:

- people that care about themselves occupy powerful 'in-charge' positions in the business (compared to leadership positions)
- people 'in-charge' milk their business to the point of insolvency or dramatic demise
- the person 'in-charge' leaves subordinates to perform the best they can, to plan and control performance
- they are at the centre of the political business arena and only respond to those who are able to make direct contact with them.

The small firm flash leader oscillates between being mean and generous, between bullying and being your friend, and between being sullen and cranky and being charming and pleasant. They also use the business as their own private ATM so become creative at accounting.

At the other end of the continuum is the money-messing megalomanic. They have the same traits as the small firm flash leader but on a much grander scale. A key difference is the money-messing megalomanic is also concerned about the business occupying an important and large part of their given market, so the business stature is important to the money-messing megalomanic.

The bullfrog lives in the shades of grey in an ethical sense and lives with dubious legal behaviours. Robert Maxwell, as well as being a drowned frog, was also a bullfrog. Conrad Black is another example of a bullfrog. Black was a Canadian newspaper 'baron' and CEO of Hollinger Inc., the third largest media group in the world.[16] In 2007 he was found guilty in the US of fraud and obstruction of justice and sentenced to 6½ years jail. It was found that he had structured deals and defrauded shareholders solely for his own benefit. After three years in jail, he was granted bail and appealed his convictions. Two of his fraud convictions were overturned, his sentence was reduced to 3½ years and he was returned to jail in 2011 but released eight months later. In 2018 Black wrote a book *Donald J. Trump: A president like no other*, and in 2019 President Trump pardoned Black, calling him a 'friend'.

Tadpoles

Tadpoles are developing frogs that fail to reach their full potential of being a fully fledged frog. In a business context they are failed start-ups, or in a large business setting are an established business brought down by a failed big new project or product.

> ❝ Tadpoles are developing frogs that fail to reach their full potential of being a fully fledged frog.

Sir Clive Sinclair was an English entrepreneur, inventor, member of British Mensa and champion poker player. However, he is

---

16 Black was actually 'entitled' to a peerage as the owner of *The Daily Telegraph*, but it was blocked by the Canadian government.

best known as an early pioneer in the personal computing and consumer electronics industry. He made the world's first slimline calculator in 1972, and in the 1980s made a range of personal computers (including the ZX Spectrum). He was heralded as the epitome of a new Elizabethan technologist, innovator, buccaneer and of success. However, he also had some failures, such as the Black Watch (a digital wristwatch), a flatscreen handheld TV, and battery-powered cars. A mere three years after being knighted for his contributions to the personal computer industry, his business – Sinclair Research – was overwhelmed by mounting debt and unsold stock from his failed projects. He ended up selling his products, patents and even his name for a mere £5m.

There are three general reasons tadpoles fail to become frogs:

1. **Over-optimism:** the business is over-optimistic about:
   - the attractiveness to customers of the product or service
   - the sales volume and/or the sales price that will be achieved
   - the speed of take up of the product or service
   - the actual cost of operations compared to the actual revenues
   - the amount of profit and cash that will be generated
   - the level of support required by suppliers and financiers
   - the ability to implement the strategic vision.

2. Failure to **perform contingency planning**.

3. A **lack of interest** by the entrepreneur or idea person in the business's success; they just want to invent or make new products and are not that interested in commercial success.

* * *

Often the traits of the different 'frogs' are a combination of different frog types. Bullfrog leaders may be CEO of a drowned frog business, or a tadpole or boiled frog business might be a pet project of a bullfrog. Robert Maxwell can be used as an example of a bullfrog, drowned frog and a tadpole business.

Most businesses focus on sales not profit

It is possible to heal the sick; it is not possible to raise the dead.

When you hear statistics like '80% of new businesses fail in the first five years', it's a wonder anyone would even start a business. Also, the businesses that do survive must be really successful; after all, you're better than 80% of the other small businesses – you're in the top 20%!

The number one reason given why new businesses fail is cash-flow – they could not generate a cash profit. I disagree – because the inability to generate cash is a symptom rather than a reason why businesses fail.

Let us look at the 20% of businesses that are continuing and con-sider if they are flourishing or in reality just surviving. What I believe is that the majority of the 20% are actually only surviving, despite the outwardly portrayed optics.

The Australia Small Business and Family Enterprise Ombudsman (ASBFEO) state that in Australia 61% of small business owners earn less than $78,000 and 45% of small businesses are failing to make a profit. A New Zealand report – 'Money Matters: Navigating the impact of economic conditions on the cashflow of New Zealand small and medium-sized businesses'[17] – found 46% of business owners and 60% of sole traders are not paying themselves in order to keep their business running.

For these business owners, while sales are increasing they believe they are successful. They have flash cars, employ lots of people, have fancy offices, but not once were they making a cash profit.

---

17 Xero, 2023.

They might not even be able to pay themselves. Their business was not flourishing – it was surviving, and then only just. I'd much rather have a business generating $1 million in sales and $200,000 in cash profit than a business generating $10 million in sales and no profit.

Sales are not as important as cash profit, though the way business is taught, either formally or informally, sales are usually the key focus. Increase turnover, look after employees, and that will translate to higher sales through happy customers. Don't stop spending on marketing else your sales funnel with dry up. This focus is a large part of why so many new businesses fail in the first five years and the ones that don't are merely surviving.

The generally accepted traditional business equation is:

Sales less expenses equals profit

What would happen though if the focus changed? Instead of sales and expenses being first, it was flipped around?

Profit equals sales less expenses

The focus is then on profit (specifically cash profit) and not on sales.

> ❝ Sales are not as important as cash profit, though the way business is taught, either formally or informally, sales are usually the key focus.

If every startup, and indeed every business, focused first on making a profit and not on sales and turnover growth, a lot more businesses would survive past the five-year mark. And not only survive but flourish. They might not be as big, and probably won't be as flashy, but the business owner will be able to go to the pub and instead of crying in their beer hit the top shelf and legitimately celebrate their achievement.

Common business failure symptoms

In a 'normal' business failure, as the business moves through the stages of underperformance, distress and crisis, the symptom that becomes most evident is problems in the financial accounts (assuming they exist, and they are complete and reasonably accurate). Keep in mind we are still in the analysis phase of the triage business turnaround, and the financial accounts are useful only to a degree for analysis as they will always be out of date.

However, in each of the stages of business decline and failure there are typical financial symptoms.

Underperformance stage symptoms

Some of the symptoms of a business underperforming are:

- revenue is stagnant or declining
- profit is stagnant or declining
- market share is stagnant or declining
- the bank is wanting more information more often, and may be seeking further security on lending.

The problem faced by many underperforming businesses is that the initial signs of underperformance are notoriously difficult to spot. It is often a multitude of small failings rather than one momentous event which is to blame for the lacklustre performance – the boiled frog.

Distress stage symptoms

Some of the symptoms of a business in the distress stage are:

- staff turnover increases
- borrowing to fund normal trading
- the business starts making regular losses to the point they become normal

- credit rating begins to fall
- forgetting that a for-profit business is to make a profit, and consider that breaking even is acceptable or a good result
- tax returns are not lodged or are late to be lodged
- relationships with banks, lenders and suppliers become strained
- like a tadpole, you put all your faith in a big project to save your business.

At this stage, financial pressures are increasing and cashflow is being stretched to breaking point.

Crisis stage symptoms

Some of the symptoms of a business in the crisis stage are:

- the Tax Office is now your major funder and may start sending recovery action notices
- letters of demand are arriving from creditors
- suppliers move to cash on delivery or reduce credit limits
- creditor days blow out past what is industry normal
- move to pay by cheque to delay payment (or to let them bounce)
- CFO resigns, leaves, or goes on extended sick leave
- rent is behind and landlord is threatening eviction.

At this stage the future of the business is on a knife's edge, teetering on the brink of being placed into a form of formal insolvency management. The swiftness and appropriateness of the action taken at this stage will determine if this occurs, or if it is the start of a successful turnaround.

These symptoms should be regarded as alarm bells, and like any situation with alarm bells, immediate action should be taken to assess the severity and timing of the impending situation. This might be assessing the business with one of the empirical tools above, or getting someone within the business to do a review of the business, including the industry and environment the business is operating in. These are subjective reviews – it also might be beneficial to get an objective review done. This might be done by your bank or accountant; however, as discussed earlier they are great at what they do but they are not experts at turning a business around that is underperforming, in decline or in crisis. For this you need to call a professional turnaround advisor. (There is a 'Getting Help' section at the end of this book with suggestions for places for getting advice.)

Results are good, taking action on the results is better. Ask yourself, 'Am I surprised at the assessment result?' If so, why? Are you working *in* your business and not *on* your business? Also ask yourself, 'What am I proactively doing to address the issues?'

Australasian cultural symptoms

Australians and New Zealanders have a relaxed and social culture, tinged with an arrogance that they can do everything and sprinkled with a 'she'll be right' attitude. They live a life valuing mateship and BBQs.

This can lead to 'seven deadly sins', or symptoms, of distressed businesses.

1. Procrastination

It's human nature to gravitate to the things you like doing or that give you pleasure and to put aside those things that don't. People do not like 'issues', and if they 'forget' them or 'put them aside' their day will be better. This might be things such as dealing with a problematic staff member, calling debtors who have not paid by the due date, or avoiding their tax and super obligations as the other creditors are standing at the reception desk demanding payment. But this procrastination does not resolve issues. It does make them worse, and issues needing attention are not dealt with. You'll actually sleep better and be more productive by tackling problems while they are manageable.

2. Mates and BBQs

Australasians love a BBQ and will do anything for their mates – the relaxed outdoor living of casually combining cooking dinner with having a beer with a mate, while simultaneously 'supervising' the kids playing in the backyard. But this relaxed, laissez faire culture being brought into the business can be fraught with danger at best, and potentially deadly. Staff are not your mates and you're not having a BBQ but running a business. Business owners need to be able to command respect from their employees, have a level of authority in the business and be attentive to the business needs and treat the business more seriously than supervising the kids at a BBQ. Failure to do so can lead to a dysfunctional workplace, poor decision-making and the risk of missing things before they become real problems.

3. Arrogance

The dictionary defines arrogance as 'an attitude of superiority manifested in an overbearing manner or in presumptuous claims or assumptions'. In distressed businesses this occurs when the business owner thinks they are the smartest person in the room, that they are the expert and no-one else understands their business. I shoot this down by asking, 'If you're the smartest person and understand everything, why is your business in distress?'[18] If you could have fixed it, you would have already. As mentioned earlier there are two truths about every business. Every business is the same and every business is different. All businesses buy and sell goods and services, must manage staff, production, workflow, have bills to pay and

---

18 The Dunning-Kruger effect is a type of cognitive bias where people with little expertise or ability assume they have superior expertise or ability. This overestimation occurs because they do not have enough knowledge to know they do not have enough knowledge. This behaviour is often evident in arrogant business owners.

receivables to collect, tax returns to submit. They are all the same. Every business also has different people, processes, culture. They have a different way of doing things, and their own 'secret sauce'. They are all different. Don't be arrogant and believe others cannot contribute or provide ideas and solutions.

4. Not seeking help early

The number one wish I have for any business in distress is get help and get help early. It benefits all stakeholders – owners, employees, customers, suppliers and other creditors. It provides more options to manage the situation for a reasonable expectation of a better outcome. It preserves value in the business. As I mentioned earlier, my client Andy had been operating his business for eight years when he contacted me: 'Hey Stephen – I have a great business, making a profit but I don't have any money'. In reality, his revenue was declining, the business was not covering overheads, he was withdrawing money from the business like it was his personal ATM, and he owed several hundred thousand to the ATO, unpaid super and various creditors. It was too late, and he ended up filing a debtor's bankruptcy petition. His problems did not start the day he contacted me, and if he had addressed the issues and sought help even 12 months prior, the situation could have been different as his options would have been greater.

> ❛ The number one wish I have for any business in distress is get help and get help early.

5. Pride

Of the seven deadly sins, theologians and philosophers reserve a special place for pride. Lust, envy, anger, greed, gluttony and sloth are all bad, the sages say, but pride is the deadliest of all, the root of all evil, and the beginning of sin. Pride is delusional, spiteful and bitter. At its root, it declares, 'I don't want God to be God. I want to be God!' There are five ways pride can destroy your business:

· **You fail to realise your business is a failure.** Just because you think your idea is ingenious, ground-breaking or unique doesn't mean others will think it is. As *Forbes* writer John Hall says, 'Don't force your pineapple burger just because you came up with it. Be real with yourself and your team; don't let your pride get in the way of your next great idea.'

· **Your ego gets out of control.** Confidence sells, ego kills. It's easy to let your ego sink your ship – and it's equally easy to see your business drown along with it. Put a process in place to test your ego.

· **You become too scared to ask for help.** You don't need to do everything yourself. Don't undervalue help. Sure, I can build a website, I can frame a wall, I can mow the lawn, and I can do bookkeeping. But I can hire others to do them, and they will be experts and do these things better and faster. Value their expertise, value your time and don't insist on doing everything yourself.

· **You make major decisions without consulting your team.** Don't fall into the trap of believing your decision-making trumps everyone else's. There is a reason you surround yourself with great people: they are there to tell you that you are crazy when you think your business should start an airport kiosk or buy from the next salesperson peddling air.

· **You do not know when it is time to exit.** In February 2023, Nicola Sturgeon – the Scottish First Minister – unexpectedly resigned. She said she knew it was the right time to leave for herself and for Scotland. Do you persevere with an idea, or in a role? Every business owner from the very first day of operating should have an exit plan. Pride will keep you in longer, and it could lead to the demise of your company.

6. Family and friends

Every business is a family business – small, big, private or public. That is because what happens at work affects you and impacts you and those at home, and vice versa. How you manage this can greatly impact your business, and everyone is different. I like leaving work at work, and continually discussing work issues creates an unbearable noise for me. My wife, though, comes home and downloads – it is her way of decompressing. Two other dangers with family and friends are the assumption that they are your customers – they are not, so run your business for your real customers. Second, unless they are a proven expert in a topic then they are not – and do not seek their advice or elevate the value of their advice (seek their support, friend-ship and love though).

7. Affluenza

Investopedia defines affluenza as 'a social condition that arises from the desire to be more wealthy or successful. It can also be defined as the inability of an individual to understand the consequences of their actions because of their social status or economic privilege.' I was at a client in a lower socioeconomic area in western Melbourne and there were a staggering number of luxury cars driving around the area and big boats being towed by expensive 4WDs with business branding. I drove around the area with my client looking at new housing developments, where the houses all had new window fittings, landscaped gardens, and I expect new furniture and fixtures and fittings inside. While I admit I am a little older than most people who live in that area, I can still remember when I was starting out like them. But what astonishes me (and yes, this is a generalisation) is the need to have the newest and the best of everything and have it now. In business, affluenza is fatal. Do you need a $90,000 4WD as your work vehicle, or would a secondhand smaller car suffice? Do you need a new machine today, or can you carry on working with the old one for a little longer? A turnaround advisor will look at short-term cashflow as one of their first and primary tasks. When I do this, requests for expenditure are often met with the question, 'Is the expenditure a like, want or need?' The process of understanding this and the discipline to live within your means will avoid problems.

Common business failure causes

'While it is the symptoms that kill you, the real cause of death is the underlying disease.'

Mark Blaney

Symptoms are outward signs of decline whereas the causes are usually more internal signs of decline.

To reiterate from earlier in this book, and my overarching tenet of business failure, there are only three reasons a business fails:

- A lack of business skills in the business.
- A lack of attention to applying business skills within the business.
- Spending the majority of the time working in the business rather than on the business.

The link between these three is they are all about *you* and how you manage the business.

There are five areas of 'causes' of normal business failure (though some also apply to 'the startup that never starts' and 'catastrophic business failure' types of business failure):[19]

- management problems
- strategic challenges
- weak financial management
- operational control
- one-off projects or circumstances.

---

19 Blaney, 2002.

Management problems

No-one likes to blame themselves, but management, management structure and management attributes are the leading cause of business failure. Some of the management problems may be:

- **Autocratic leadership:** The owner or CEO has total control over all decisions and is absolute that they must be obeyed; there is no debate or discussion, and the autocrat is driving the business over a cliff.

- **Lack of leadership:** If the business is led by an autocrat the 'management team' is usually a bunch of 'yes-people', drones – or both! Leadership needs to be strong, where everyone's role and opinion is meaningful, everyone makes a contribution and is recognised. However, where leadership is weak, the business is like a headless chicken.

- **Limited experience:** The management team or board comprises people with a limited range and depth of skill and experience. For example, a construction business might comprise the owner/CEO, the sales manager, the construction team and the operations manager. They consider other skills incidental as 'they have got this far without them', and also do not see the need for those skills or want to incur the expense to gain them. They might also consider that doing so will dilute their own power, influence, control or status on the board and/or the business.

- **Not accepting or seeking external advice:** If you consider other skills incidental at the management or board level of the business then it will be even more so elsewhere in the business; for example, if there is not a strong financial management person in the management group, the value placed on financial management at lower levels will be low and the business will certainly not be willing to seek or acquire strong financial management advice externally (or want to pay for it).

- **Failure of the management structure to change as the business changes:** The structure and size of the management team needs to reflect the size and requirements of the business. A small startup business does not require a board of 12; conversely, as the business grows a more professional and functional board and management team may be required with more delegation of control.

- **Poor or no succession planning:** When I was growing up, advertising was newspaper ads, pamphlets in the mailbox, and radio and TV advertising. Nowadays, advertising is all online. In 30 years' time will the management team be headed by the same leaders? Probably not – you need to allow for generational change in the world.

- **Civil war:** A dispute between the board and management team, or within the management team, if not addressed immediately will lead to a destructive business failure.

- **Poor or no accountability:** In the movie *The Shawshank Redemption*, there is a scene where Morgan Freeman's character Otis 'Red' Redding is speaking to Tim Robbins's character Andy Dufresne. They're both inmates at Shawshank State Prison, and Red is suggesting to Andy that the hope of release or escape will drive a man mad, as it's immensely unlikely to come true. Failure to face up to business problems, thinking 'everyone in the industry is in the same boat' and there is 'nothing we can do' is putting faith in the 'turnaround fairy' – which does not exist!

- **Family issues:** Yes, I've said before that every business is a family business. In the causes of business failure, a business that is run for the benefit of the family foremost and not the interests of the business as an entity will suffer.

- **No profit focus:** As discussed earlier, the business purpose is to make a profit, and the focus needs to be on making a profit.

- **Troubling syndromes:** There is the 'bluebottle' or 'Oh my god we killed Kenny!' syndrome – where management runs on total chaos and that is their preferred mode of operation. The 'goldfish memory syndrome' is where management easily loses their thoughts and focus, and forgets things (like filing tax returns and paying super). Or the 'ostrich syndrome' – otherwise known as 'head in the sand syndrome' – whereby the management team avoid negative information and fail to deal with problems.

Strategic challenges

In the preface I wrote the 'reasons' for business failure are usually outwardly, externally focused challenges. There are also usually many opportunities presented to the business. It is, however, how the business responds and adapts internally to the challenges and opportunities, or doesn't, that will cause business failure:[20]

---

20 For an example of strategic challenges causing business failure, review British retailer Marks & Spencer. There were several factors that contributed to Marks & Spencer's business crisis:

Competition: M&S faced increased competition from a range of retailers, including fast fashion brands and online retailers. These competitors were able to offer lower prices and more diverse product ranges, which made it harder for M&S to attract and retain customers.

Failure to adapt to changing consumer preferences: M&S failed to keep up with changing consumer preferences, particularly among younger shoppers. Customers wanted more variety, trendier styles and a more seamless online shopping experience, all of which M&S struggled to provide.

Poor management decisions: M&S made some poor management decisions, such as expanding into overseas markets without fully understanding the local market dynamics, and investing heavily in large out-of-town stores at a time when customers were increasingly shopping online.

Decline in food sales: M&S has traditionally been known for its high-quality food offerings, but its food sales declined due to increased competition from other supermarkets, as well as changing consumer preferences towards healthier, more sustainable options.

Supply chain issues: M&S faced supply chain issues, including inefficient stock management and delays in introducing new products, which led to reduced sales and profits.

- **Failure to recognise and adapt to industry changes and the market.** In all industries, things evolve. In retail it is evident, in fashion trends, in transport we are seeing the evolution to electric vehicles after decades with internal combustion engines.

- **The end of natural lifecycles.** Some products' and business's lifecycles end or fade away. Think of listening to music – from in person, to wireless radio, to tape decks, to CDs, to iPods, to smartphones and watches. Products and services should be regularly reviewed to make sure your business is not left behind, and to allow your business to reinvent it's offering or offer the next 'big thing'.

- **Failure to prepare for business cycles.** Economies go through periods of growth and recession, and industries go through cycles or phases; for example, in Australia there was an enormous growth period in the mining sector, followed by a period of consolidation and less development. As the economy slows, do you start building up working capital reserves or invest in a high-cost discretionary spend item?

- **Failure to manage change.** Managing change should be an ongoing and normal part of business. Failure to continuously manage change leads to having to manage a big change rather than small incremental changes, which is much more disruptive and far riskier.

- **Poor cost structure.** Being uncompetitive on costs is a surefire way to business failure. There may be reasons for higher costs such as scale (you manufacture 100 widgets and your competitor manufacturers 100,000) or location (you are in Sydney versus a competitor in Hobart where rents are lower). Of course, this is relevant for like-for-like products or services, and if they aren't you may get away with higher costs if you can demonstrate a higher value and the customer values that too.

- **Failure to invest in the future.** When a business is in distress, cash is tight and the management and/or owners gravitate to working in the business to generate more cash. However, at the same time they are not devoting time and resources to developing business skills, training their staff, developing products and service offerings, and nurturing contacts – to the detriment of their long-term survival.

- **Focusing on the new and forgetting the old.** As a parent it would frustrate me that kids love new toys, and other kids' toys, and quickly forget their favourite toy from last week. When developing a new product or service offering, do not neglect the old product or service offerings; after all, they are or were providing the funding and opportunity for your new offering and you need to make sure that cash continues coming in at the same rate.

- **Overexposure.** Overexposure (a.k.a. all eggs in one basket) can be in many forms – overexposure to a client or set of clients, overexposure to a new project, overexposure to a new product or service offering, or 'betting' on one acquisition or one big, new contract. Overexposure can tie up both cash and time. Overexposure is prevalent in the construction industry, especially in small businesses that subcontract for larger businesses. Often the failure of the larger business is like a 'pebble in the pond' and the impact flows to the subcontractors, resulting in their business distress. Additionally, reliance on the overexposed product, service, contract or acquisition places your business's fate in the hands of others, and reduces your power and influence (for example, you become too susceptible to pricing from a supplier).

Weak financial management

No matter what industry your business is in, or how big or small it is, or the corporate structure of the business, good financial management is a necessity and a fundamental part of the business. It's not okay to ignore it or downplay its importance. It might not be something you like focusing on, but ignore it at your peril as it is akin to driving blind. Financial management is the backbone of every business, and if you want your business to survive, be sustainable or grow, you need to understand your finances.

I was having a hard discussion with a client around their lack of focus on financial management and ensuring information input into their accounting software was consistently correct. The response was if the office manager was not capable they would outsource this task to a bookkeeper or accountant. They missed the point – this was not the solution to the problem. The problem was a lack of attention, diligence and focus on understanding the financial information and being able to understand what it is telling them, and in turn being able to make smart, profitable business decisions.

There are three main areas of financial control problems:

1. **Control:** Lack of financial controls can lead to catastrophic consequences for the business, such as fraud and increased debt.

2. **Information:** Reliable financial information is vital to making decisions to save a distressed business. Information needs to be timely and accurate. I went to a medium-sized business to work on a turnaround in November and they still had not completed the June management reports (let alone the end-of-financial-year statutory and tax reports). They had a CPA qualified Chief Financial Officer, but this person did not know how to do a balance sheet reconciliation, what their debtor days were or even have an accurate tax liability figure. They were waiting for their tax accountant to do their tax return the following April. Essentially they were 'running blind', with no timely or accurate financial information.

3. **Management:** There are consequences of not properly managing the business finances:

   - *Not getting paid, or not getting paid in a timely manner:*
     The client in the example above had debtor days of 102; that is, the average time from making a sale to getting the money owed was 102 days. By working with the client, in the space of a fortnight their debtor days reduced to 67 days. This created a $3.2m improvement in their cash position.

   - *Inventory problems:* Another large client I worked with had $150m in inventory and a broken (and, quite frankly, stupid for them) procurement process whereby as soon as an item was sold it would automatically be replaced. As a result, there was $30m in stock that had been there for more than three years, written off in the accounting profit and loss, but utilising funding (they could scrap it and would have an immediate cash boost). They also had 9,000 stock line items but in reality only sold about 2,500 stock line items.

   - *Poor funding structures:* A mechanical engineering client had a van that was going to require several thousands of dollars to maintain it, plus potential downtime both fixing it and with the van out of operation. Their options were to fix the van or sell the van and borrow money to buy a new (or newer) van. One of the two decision-makers said let's just fix it, until I got them to work out the cost and then how they were going to fund that cost. I then asked them to do the same with borrowing for a newer van over four years and they could sell the old van immediately as is. The point being, you need to consider the appropriateness of any funding. As an aside, they did go with borrowing money for a newer van but in the process struggled to get finance from a major lender so looked at second- and third-tier lenders. Most of these lenders' interest rates were two to three times that of the major lender, though they did end up finding one only 70 basis points higher than the major lender.

- *Being over-leveraged:* Let's assume there are two businesses with the same turnover in the same industry – one with net assets of $100m and it makes $10m profit a year, and the second business has net assets of $20m and makes a net profit of $15m. To the outsider the second business is more profitable. Then there is a 'shock': rampant inflation, labour shortages or supply chain problems (or all three at once). Which is the better business to be able to sustain the pressures of decreasing profit, higher interest costs and continuing capital repayments? Which would have the ability to get funding to assist them through this period? The first business. Over-leveraged businesses are over-exposed businesses.

- *Over trading:* This is also known as growing too quickly. Growth is good, but growing faster than the supply of funds will result in cash shortages. Growth needs to be managed on the funding side too. I use an analogy of property investing. People when buying their first home are restricted by interest repayments, serviceability requirements and the deposit they have as to how much they can spend on a house. In a business, interest repayments are the same, serviceability is free cashflow from business operations and the deposit is the strength of the balance sheet. After a few years the house owner decides to get a bigger house (they may have a growing family, or want a swimming pool or a bigger garden). The homeowner must pass the same criteria they did for their first house to fund the move to the bigger house. But the business wanting to grow, or 'just is' growing, or develops a new product or service offering, can just do so – but should have the same discipline as the house owner and ensure they can actually fund that growth.

- *Poor expense management:* When I first went to my mechanical engineering client there were two expense items that stood out to me straight away.[21] The first was entertainment expenses that amounted to over $5,000 annually. When I queried what this was, I was told it was Friday lunches for the staff – only $100 a week. The second expense item was consumables – rags, oil, masking tape and so on, and the total was over $20k annually. Now this business was losing $100k annually. We made two immediate changes that did not impact the business operations. First the Friday lunches stopped, and the second was a 2% of labour consumables charge on every invoice. So 25% of this client's losses were resolved in 10 minutes through expenses management. A little later in the turnaround we implemented an expense decision process: ask if the expense is a *like*, a *want* or a *need*. Needs that were in the budget were approved, but if they were not in the budget, they may get approved and would also require an explanation as to why they were not in the budget. Likes would not be approved and wants would need justification for the expense before it would be considered.[22]

Operational control

How well do the functions of the business operate? Are they efficient and are they operating as expected?

Inefficient operations can occur in several areas:

- **Production inefficiency:** This may be through poor factory layout, lack or inappropriateness of organised systems or processes, equipment that is no longer fit for purpose,

---

21 This client had annual turnover of around $350k and three staff.
22 This client did not have a budget at the start of this process.

or a production range that is too broad and does not meet customer demands.

- **Quality control:** Can you replicate your product or service to a consistent level of quality each and every time?
- **Ineffective salesforce or processes**: Is your marketing and sales team working collegiately and effectively, and are they supported by an efficient distribution system?

Larry the Landscaper is super busy and works around 100 hours each week. He gets up, goes to work, comes home and either falls asleep in front of the TV or drags himself straight to bed. Larry's philosophy for coping with the workload (or not coping, as probably is the case) is 'just do it' rather than figuring out how to get the work done through using other people who use innovative systems to produce consistent results. Now I concede theory is easy and practice is hard, but it takes continual steps forward to climb a mountain.

Often there is a lot of pushback to begin systemising a business, but it is the journey and process of trying to that yields the greatest benefit for a struggling business. Through the process, issues are going to be identified and thought is going to be given to how to resolve those issues.

Staff issues are also a result of a lack of operational control, specifically the 'soft skills' and role suitability. How well do you understand the culture of your business, what motivates your staff, what characteristics are best suited for every role, how do you reward your staff, what is your management style, and how does it work with your staff? Do you have 'round' pegs in 'round' holes? Do you know which of your staff are 'round' and which are 'square'? Are there systems in place that 'round' and 'square' staff use to complement each other?

One-off project or circumstances

Often a big project or special circumstance can be the 'straw that breaks the camel's back'. This might be something such as moving to larger premises, implementing a new inventory or accounting system, merging or acquiring a business, or launching a new product or service offering.

With existing weaknesses in management, strategic management and financial and operational control, big projects and special circumstances can exacerbate these weaknesses. As such, they are often a fundamental cause of business failure.

Part II

EMERGENCY PHASE

S o far everything discussed has been on assessing the situation – the causes of decline, the assessment of the business, its staff and management, the severity of the overall problem, and the options available. This time spent on the Analysis phase is important. Einstein said, 'If I had an hour to solve a problem, I'd spend 55 minutes thinking about it and five minutes thinking of solutions.'

Chapter 3

Where the turnaround begins

There are six steps to problem solving:

1. **Define the problem:** Look at the context, the background and symptoms. Then the implications of the problem, who is affected, and how urgent/important it is to resolve.

2. **Determine the root cause(s) of the problem:** Explore what has caused the problem.

3. **Develop alternative solutions:** Look at all the options and eliminate any that are not effective for dealing with the symptoms and the root cause.

4. **Select a solution:** Narrow the alternatives down to one course of action.

5. **Implement the solution:** Agree on a team, a plan, actions, timing and milestones.

6. **Evaluate outcomes:** Monitor the project to ensure it is effective and desired outcomes are being achieved.

So far, this book has addressed the first two steps and has covered the first '55 minutes of thinking'. Now arguably the hardest part begins – the 'Emergency phase'. This is where the turnaround begins.

The emergency phase of business triage is all about doing what is necessary for the business to survive – nothing more, nothing less.

> ❝ The emergency phase of business triage is all about doing what is necessary for the business to survive – nothing more, nothing less.

Most aspects of a turnaround are not done in isolation, rather steps and tasks are done concurrently. Turnaround planning and strategy actually begins in the Analysis phase, occurs in the Emergency phase, and continues in the Crisis Stabilisation and Growth phases.

A turnaround strategy is simply a process or set of actions to transform the business from a crisis or distressed situation to a stable, profitable situation. It is the unwinding of the actions and decisions made earlier that resulted in the current situation and implementing actions and making decisions that will transform the business into a profitable one.

Broadly, there are four turnaround management strategies:

- **Retrenchment:** A range of short-term actions. There are process changes but no business structure changes.
- **Repositioning:** An entrepreneurial strategy that looks to generate revenue by changing the product portfolio, the market position, or through new products or services. This will be looked at in the Crisis Stabilisation phase and is more strategic in focus.
- **Replacement:** A clean out of the current management team and replacement with a management team experienced in turnarounds. This will be looked at in the Crisis Stabilisation phase and is more strategic in focus.

- **Renewal:** Looks at longer term actions and ongoing success of the business. This begins in the Crisis Stabilisation phase and continues in the Growth phase and is strategic in focus.

The turnaround plan

A turnaround plan is a written document and a roadmap to save the business. It is a key requirement to communicate with stakeholders and to convince them about the turnaround. It needs to be done and done well, so it takes time and effort. It also needs to be brutally honest, outlining how you arrived at the current situation and how you will stay in business while the turnaround is being conducted. Every turnaround plan is different, as each distressed business and situation is different.

Different turnaround practitioners have different approaches to a turnaround plan. Some may develop a written plan before commencing any actions. My personal strategy is to write the turnaround plan as part of the Analysis and Emergency phases. I do this for two reasons: firstly, the information I need for the plan comes from doing these two phases, and secondly, the Analysis and Emergency phases are about 'buying time' to execute the turnaround plan. It's all great to have a plan but it's no good if you do not have the time to execute it.

A turnaround plan is different to a generic business plan. It:

- includes actions that cover a short period – maybe three months
- requires constant monitoring, updating and extensive analysis
- is compiled at a time of heightened financial and emotional stress
- requires judgement, experience and the good 'ole gut feeling as perfect information is seldom available.

There is little or no margin for error – bad decisions can be fatal to a distressed business.

The plan covers the following areas.

Background of the business

Different stakeholders come with different levels and views about the business. The background section puts all stakeholders in a situation where they are familiar with how and when the business was formed, what it does, the ownership structure and the key personnel in the business and the turnaround.

Stakeholders

There are many groups of stakeholders (as discussed later) and their trust and support are key to the success of the turnaround. Identify and prioritise stakeholders as per the section later, and include this analysis in the turnaround plan.

Why your business is in distress

The Analysis phase covers the question of why the business is in distress. The turnaround plan documents this and then turns this into usable information. Cover the areas of external factors, the operational management factors, finance, sales and marketing, and family vs business. In this section of the plan, consider how you are going to mitigate the negative impacts of these factors, how you will repair the damage that has already occurred, and how you are going to prevent these factors from reoccurring.

Vision, mission and goals

This will be covered in more detail in the strategic focus section. This section analyses the current strategic vision (if there was one).

Usually, distressed businesses do not have a strategic plan, and if they do, it is left in a drawer and never looked at.

Financing the turnaround

The harsh reality is a turnaround costs money, and paradoxically the distressed business is cash poor. But the stakeholders all need to know how the turnaround will be funded before it proceeds. The financing also can determine the options and strategies available. However, there is a silver lining in determining how the turnaround will be financed – it often uncovers and fixes the issues that led to the problems in the first place.

Cash

Cash is discussed in detail below. As cash is the lifeblood of the business, how it is managed needs to be in the turnaround plan.

Financial control

Once cash is under control and the cash bleed has stopped, strong financial control is vital to keep the cash flowing and the bleeding stemmed. This is discussed in detail later in this part.

Debt restructure

It is almost certain that a distressed business will have debt – and lots of it. Debt may be in many forms: bank and financial institution debt, creditors and suppliers, unpaid taxes, unpaid employee entitlements such as superannuation, and monies from shareholders, family and related parties. Often it is a combination of many of these. The turnaround plan needs to include how to reduce the debt and how to structure the debt, so it is manageable and efficient for the business. If you cannot restructure the debt the chances of the turnaround being successful are low. This may mean negotiating payment plans, and working out plans with creditors and investors. Most creditors, including the Tax Office, will support plans that show them getting paid – eventually – and if you execute the plan religiously.

> ❝ If you cannot restructure the debt the chances of the turnaround being successful are low.

Working capital management

Working capital is the amount of current assets less the amount of current liabilities. It includes items such as cash in the bank, accounts receivable and inventory on the asset side of the equation, and accounts payable, tax obligations and employee obligations on the liabilities side of the equation. Even growing businesses can end up in financial distress, and this is usually because working capital management was poor. The focus was on revenue growth and sales, and attention was not given to the timing of payments to employees and creditors, and the inventory levels and management, and the collection of cash from debtors. The plan needs to include how working capital is managed, and is discussed in detail in the cash section later in the book.

Evaluation of products and services

This is usually not something I do in the Emergency phase but do as part of the strategic focus during the Crisis Stabilisation phase. This is because evaluation of products and services is more holistic than just cash and if a product or service is making money or not. Also, if say 90% of the business is profitable and 10% not, eliminating the unprofitable part of the business may not fundamentally change the nature of the business. If though 90% is unprofitable, the question might be 'why are we in this business at all?' That is a lot larger question than how are we going to survive long enough to make strategic decisions.

Brand and image evaluation

Again, while important to include in the turnaround plan, this is not an activity I necessarily undertake in the Emergency phase. It is included as it is difficult to execute a turnaround when the outside image (and I'd argue the inside image) is of a business on the way out. If you watch *Ramsay's Kitchen Nightmares*, you will see Gordon Ramsay focus on three things – the food, the staff and how they feel about the restaurant (see the next part of the turnaround plan), and then he has a team come and redecorate the restaurant at the end. But the first part is the food and the staff and owners, not the paint and curtains – though that is important.

Employees

People management is critical in a turnaround. A concept to consider is reciprocity. Reciprocity is the natural tendency to reciprocate in kind when people act towards us in a certain way. If a business is loyal to its staff, it is likely the staff will react in kind and be loyal to the business. Likewise, burn or betray your employees and they will likely do the same to the business. The turnaround plan needs to articulate how people will be brought together to put the business back on track. Get everyone pulling together and a lot can be achieved.

SWOT analysis

A SWOT (strengths, weaknesses, opportunities, threats) analysis creates a profile of the business.

Executive summary

This is the first part of the turnaround plan but the last part you write. It provides an overview of the plan and aims to convince people to read the rest of the plan. Do not put lots of detail or feel you have to make it a prescribed length, but it needs to be polished and well written.

Not all turnaround leaders are talented writers. Your turnaround plan and how it is presented though is paramount for building support. Get the plan checked for spelling and grammatic errors, and formatting. The turnaround plan for the reader is a mirror of the writer. Sloppy writing might suggest sloppy analysis. Spelling and punctuation errors might suggest a lack of attention to detail, and so you might not have the required attention to business details. I was working with a client that had engaged former world champion aerial skier Jacqui Cooper's business Champion Events to do some management training. She made a comment about messy cars in the carpark, and untidy offices – that these were indicators of how people think. A messy car or office indicated being disorganised and lacking detail of thought. While this was a generalisation, it stuck with me, and now when I first turn up to a client's premises, I am looking at tidiness as an indication of how they think.

How to finance the turnaround

If you could have turned your business around by yourself, without help, you would have already. Unfortunately, to be successful with the turnaround you are going to require expert help. Turnarounds are medium-term engagements and not discrete tasks. Turnaround advisors need to be paid, and the costs need to be factored into the turnaround plan as they need to be financed. Include in the turnaround plan how much money you'll need, when you will need it, and how it will be used. It is always a good indication of how committed the owners are to the turnaround if they stop when they understand the turnaround advisor's cost. However, two thoughts: the turnaround advisor is an investment not a cost, and the investment will be outweighed by the return on investment. Consider my client Andy again – within an hour of being engaged I had generated more income than my engagement fee. Secondly – banks are more likely to support, and possibly fund, the turnaround when you engage a turnaround advisor with a proven record in successful turnarounds.

The turnaround team

This is one of the most critical success factors in a turnaround: the team.

The first decision with team selection is who the turnaround leader will be. Usually, the turnaround leader is the Chief Executive Officer. They then need to select a team to focus on the turnaround, which is often a combination of internal and external people.

There are two common mistakes in team formation:

- **'We can do it ourselves.'** Well, no ... you cannot – because if you could, you would have done it already. Einstein also said, 'We can't solve problems by using the same kind of thinking we used when we created them.' You and your team may have the skills, but the skills might not be the complete set of skills required. Your people may lack the experience of a turnaround, and they may not have the passion, enthusiasm, desire, time and focus required to execute a turnaround successfully.

- **'Let's use the accountant and lawyer we always use.'** Turnaround is a dirty business and requires people to roll their sleeves up and get among the workings of the business. And, like the above, your usual accountant and lawyer might have skills, but the skills might not be the complete set of skills required, and they may lack the experience of a turnaround and may not have the passion, enthusiasm, desire and focus required to execute a turnaround successfully.

I had a client who had a fast-growing business – 50% growth each of the previous two years. They had a CFO, they had an external accounting advisor and external legal advisor. They had two shareholders with many years' experience in their industry. They had a large contract dispute, and together with the fast growth, this had caused major working capital and liquidity problems. This meant they got behind with tax payments – they used the Australian Taxation Office as a bank. We started the turnaround process by identifying the problems and causes, and put a plan in place to execute the turnaround. At this stage our contract was terminated. Why? Because they felt they could do it themselves and 'save on the cost'.

But the lawyers managing the contract dispute were employment lawyers not commercial lawyers with deep experience in their sector, their accountant was a sole practitioner that was not on top of their tax obligations. The CFO was terminated (at our suggestion), as this person had been making some unauthorised transactions, had misled the board, and five months after year end still did not have the financial results ready. He and his team did not know how to do a balance sheet reconciliation or calculate debtor days. His replacement ended up getting pulled away from what was core to focus on other things that 'were more important'. The turnaround never happened – they carried on doing what they had always done. The situation got worse. With the right team, the right skills, and the right amount of focus on the turnaround, this company would have been in a healthy position and growing.

I have deliberately set my turnaround and crisis management firm, Byronvale Advisors, to operate using a polymathic consulting model. Instead of having a set of employees each with a discrete set of skills so that we would have to find work that matches those individuals and those skills, we look at the client and engagement individually. We build a turnaround and crisis management team based on the client, the client's and the client's advisors' skills, and the time and focus of the client. Our aim is to have a team with the correct skills and experience required, that can be hands-on in the process. Build a team of the right people, at the right place, and at the right time. Not only does this help ensure a successful outcome, but it is also usually far cheaper and faster.

Chapter 4

Cash

When a gravely sick patient arrives at the emergency trauma department, the paramedic briefs the physicians on the state of the patient's heart and brain. They will tell the doctors the GCS (Glasgow Coma Scale) score and the heart rate and arrhythmia of the heart. The heart and brain are the most important organs in the body. Neither the brain nor the heart work without the other. The heart and brain are also linked by blood vessels and nerves.

Likewise, when we first see a business in distress or crisis, we are given an assessment of the 'heart' and 'brain' of the business. They tell us about the business – why it exists, the products, the market, the concept – the heart – and what the business does and why it is unique or famous – the brains.

What we do not usually get told is the status of the cash – the 'blood vessels and nerves' of the business that link the brain and the heart. Like blood that courses through our veins, cash circulates through the business and keeps everything functioning.

'Never take your eyes off the cashflow, because it is the lifeblood of the business.'

Sir Richard Branson

We assess the 'brain' and 'heart' of the business when we decide to take on a turnaround engagement; our first task is to assess the cash situation. We look at cash in two timeframes. The first is short-term cash, with two important objectives in mind. Is there enough cash to pay wages? Staff (and cash) are the two most important assets of the business. Secondly, is there enough cash to manage the working capital? Can the main creditors be paid, or paid enough, to stop them commencing formal insolvency proceedings?

In most turnaround situations, cash management takes precedence over everything else – that's how important cash is. Without cash the business will not survive, or at the very least not survive long enough to effect a successful turnaround.

> In most turnaround situations, cash management takes precedence over everything else – that's how important cash is.

Cash management is hard – and is usually a cultural shock to the business and management team. It involves hard decisions, and is often received with a healthy dose of complaints, scepticism and apprehension.

There are four steps involved in turnaround cash management:

1. assessment
2. planning
3. controls
4. rationing.

Cash assessment

Fred Adler, a famous US venture capitalist, said, 'Happiness is a positive cashflow'. Cashflow, as defined in the Cambridge Dictionary, is 'the amount of money moving into and out of a business'. Think of cashflow like putting petrol in your car – you fill up the car's tank with petrol, and it empties as you drive. The goal, however, is to have enough petrol in your tank so you never run on empty – or in this case, having a positive cashflow.

❝ Just because you are profitable does not mean you have a positive cashflow.

This positive cashflow should be a goal for all businesses – spending less money than you generate. Just because you are profitable does not mean you have a positive cashflow. It's paradoxical! In the best of times, you might have the worst of times. You might build things two months in advance and not receive the monies for sales for six months.

And just as an aside, even growing businesses can have negative cashflows – and can become insolvent. I have seen many companies grow fast but struggle to pay their bills (including taxes and employee entitlements). What had not received the necessary attention was how the business was funding the growth. These businesses usually try to grow with inadequate cash reserves at the start. Profitable companies can also have mismatched cash-to-cash cycles. This measures the days cash is tied up in the main cash-producing and cash-consuming areas: receivables, payables and inventory. In most cases, the lower the number, the better. Often, the cash-to-cash cycle is much longer than the accounting recognition, so while it looks like you are making a profit, there is a mismatch between the profit and when cash leaves and enters the business.

Cash analysis of financial information is important. To most SMEs, financial information is not given much attention. It's an afterthought, and is often only the information compiled by the tax accountant when (or if) the business submits their tax return; for example, the profit and loss statement and balance sheet statement. By this stage the financial information is out of date and meaningless in assessing cash and cashflow. Profit also does not equate to solvency – you can make profit and have solvency problems.

The two most useful financial reports – in my opinion – are the cashflow forecast and the cashflow statement. These reports are forward-looking and current reports.

Cashflow forecast

I find the cashflow forecast the most useful report for the day-to-day management of a business. Unlike most accounting reports that review what has occurred in the past, such as the profit and loss statements or balance sheets, the cashflow forecast is a proactive tool.

To build a cashflow forecast is relatively easy. Start with your current bank balance, add all certain inflows for cash, and sub-tract all certain outflows of cash. You should do this based on the incremental period that you choose – daily, weekly or monthly. It's important to only include inflows and outflows that you are certain will occur – that you can bank on (excuse the pun).

Most accounting software packages can produce a simple cash-flow forecast; however, this should be used only as a starting point.

Here are some questions to ask when building a cashflow forecast:

- Are all the invoices in the accounting system? (Make sure they are not sitting unopened on someone's desk or filed in a drawer or wastepaper basket.)

- Are the payment and receipt dates reflective not just of the payment terms but of when they are expected to be paid and received?
- Are all cash items (GST, wages, taxes, superannuation) included? Put the GST-inclusive amounts in your cashflow forecast and not the GST-exclusive amounts that you have in your financial plan or profit and loss statement.

Start with the cash items you are certain of. It may not be possible to know actual future sales cashflows; if you must put projected sales cashflows in the forecast, do so conservatively and notate your assumptions.

The cashflow forecast's great use is showing where the cashflow gaps are – the crunch points.

Cashflow statement

Unlike the cashflow forecast, the cashflow statement looks at how the business has funded itself over a period. Consequently, the cashflow statement is often included in financial statements.

The cashflow statement is broken into three areas of cash movement:

- **Cashflow from operations:** This is the actual money your business generated from core business activities. This will show if the current core business activities generated a positive or negative cashflow. It excludes accounts receivables and depreciation so is a good indicator if the cash-to-cash cycle is too long and there are delays receiving monies from customers. Historical reports are best looked at and compared to regular intervals rather than just a one-off. The trend is the real power.
- **Cashflow from investing:** This is the money that was spent on infrastructure – plant, equipment, IT systems, property. This is important as it may help explain a large decrease in the cash that

is not actually a day-to-day business expense but an investment in the business's future.

- **Cashflow from financing:** This includes loan repayments, interest, monies from or to the business owners, and loans. This helps understand each type of cash injection or withdrawal and gives a basis to decide if they are healthy or not. Again, the greatest benefit is comparing periods.

I believe one of the biggest – and most overlooked – benefits of analysing cashflow through a cashflow forecast or cashflow statement is that management and business owners gain deep insight into their business. This may be understanding process issues, discovering incorrect payment terms on invoices, finding said invoices are not funded appropriately, or their working capital does not support their sales strategy. So apart from avoiding a cash squeeze, the information garnered will help you run your business better.

Cash planning

The cashflow forecast and cashflow statement provide us with the information to make some cashflow plans. They provide a picture of the real and current cash situation. The cashflow forecast is then modified with initiatives to plug the gaps and secure the cashflow health of the business. When doing this planning, each initiative should be looked at independently of the others so the effects of each are clear.

There are five main short-term cash-generation initiatives:

- debtor reduction
- creditor extensions
- inventory reduction
- expenditure management
- short-term financial support.

Debtor reduction

Using a simple formula, known as Debtor Days, we work out the average number of days it takes customers to pay their invoices. The formula is:

(Average debtors) ÷ (Annual sales) × 365

For example, $105,000 Average debtors, $1,000,000 Annual sales: 105,000 ÷ 1,000,000 × 365 = 38.

Using this example, it takes on average 38 days from when a customer is invoiced to pay you. So, if you could halve the number of days in Debtor Days you could 'find' over $50,000 in cash. As mentioned earlier I had a client with $32 million in sales and Debtor Days at 102 days. Very quickly we put in some effort and focused the staff on debtor collections, and within a couple of weeks got the Debtor Days to 67 days. This was a $3.2 million improvement in their cash forecast in a fortnight! Generally, the smaller the Debtor Days the better.

Debtor Days should be assessed against the industry standard; for example, if your business is in the construction industry, and it is normal that contract terms are 60 days, this is the benchmark or target number of days that your Debtor Days are to be assessed against. Trends in Debtor Days should also be looked at. If the Debtor Days are moving out over time, that could indicate a problem with your focus on collections, but also might be a result of something larger such as an economic slowdown. An economic or industry factor would still indicate more focus needs to be on collecting debts.

The other useful piece of debtor information is an Aged Debtors report. The Aged Debtors report lists all debtors and then 'ages' the invoices into buckets: current, one month, two months, three months, greater than three months. This quickly identifies if there might be problems with a particular customer. Problems may be with either party; for example, there may be quality or delivery problems resulting in the customer delaying payment, or the customer may have their own financial problems or staffing issues. It is usual in a turnaround that these have gone in the 'too hard' box, and the business has failed to address them.

Looking at Debtor Days and cash collection can take up most of a turnaround team's time in the first few days. Also, a team led by the turnaround manager is usually established to focus solely on debt recovery. It is a task where the old debts and debts in dispute are removed from those usually responsible. This circumvents the self-interest of the usual parties; for example, the finance department and sales department.

There are initiatives that may aid in accelerating cash collections on future debts. The sales/production team may consider trying to persuade customers to pay a deposit (or the whole amount in full) upon placing the order. They could also prioritise production and sales to the better-paying customers. Slightly harder is renegotiating trading terms with customers. I once had a client whose largest customer had trading terms 90 days from end of month, and a sales margin of 2%. My client was losing money on this customer – as the funding costs were greater than the sales margin – let alone all the overheads and return on equity. Then there are expensive initiatives such as offering a discount for early settlement on good debts, and factoring arrangements.

Creditor extensions

For a business in distress, extending credit terms is far harder than reducing Debtor Days and needs to be handled sensitively and strategically. Knowing your suppliers and understanding the relationship and their issues is critical. The last thing you need is to be cut off by a critical supplier or to be put on cash-only terms, worsening your cash position further.

Like with Debtor Days and Aged Debtors, we start by looking at the average time the business is paying creditors, and the age of creditors.

The Creditor Days formula is:

$$\textbf{(Average creditors)} \div \textbf{(Annual sales)} \times \textbf{365}$$

For example, $165,000 Average creditors, $1,000,000 Annual sales: 165,000 ÷ 1,000,000 × 365 = 60.

Again, this ratio needs to look at a trend and be compared to industry benchmarks. A declining ratio may indicate you have a worsening working capital position. This could be due to a decreasing stock turn or lengthening number of debtor days.

Like the Aged Debtors report, the Aged Creditors report lists all creditors and then 'ages' the invoices into buckets: current, one month, two months, three months, greater than three months. The interesting thing about this report is that apart from indicating the suppliers that the business pays fastest or slowest and the quantum of the debt to them, it also indicates the importance of particular creditors to the business and the relationship with them.

Like with debtor collections, assign a 'point person' to manage the negotiations with creditors. Understand the creditor book – use the 80:20 rule and sort the creditors by amount as well as creditor days. Understand the process for payments – are they automatic payments, are some paid ahead of the due date due to a relationship issue, who is driving the decision of which creditors to pay and when? Look at moving purchases to on consignment and look at alternative suppliers that may offer better payment terms.

Nearly always the largest creditor or the one that is most overdue is the Tax Office. In Australia, the Australian Taxation Office (ATO) is colloquially known as the fifth bank. They are also the creditor responsible for initiating the most insolvency actions, so they need to be managed delicately. Like most people and businesses, they do not like surprises, so there are a couple of actions that can be undertaken to avoid this and to protect your business and the directors.

The way the ATO gets information is through tax return lodgements. Having lodgements up to date will give you a platform to negotiate payment plans and interest remissions, and may delay or change the severity of insolvency actions such as director penalty notices, garnishee orders or windup notices. The struggle for the turnaround manager is getting the lodgements up to date, as the financial data used for the lodgements may be incomplete and/or inaccurate, therefore they have to spend time and resources getting this data and information. Ensure all lodgements are up to date – even ones that you may not consider core, such as fringe benefit tax returns and taxable payments annual report (TPAR).

Lease payments are also usually a large expense, either for the premises where you do business and house inventory or undertake production, or for large and key machinery. Lease payments are notoriously difficult to renegotiate, and non-payment can quickly stop the business from operating.

Inventory reduction

A large business that was a client (let's call them 'Client A') imported and distributed products, as well as manufactured some products. They had a whole procurement team and had built their own procurement system. There were flaws in the system; the biggest was it would automatically reorder a product as soon as it was sold. So, they sold a product, and it was the first time in three years, and the system went and reordered the product. They had 9,500 stock line items in inventory, but only 'regularly' sold about 2,500 items.

Fortunately, the products were not fungible and did not deteriorate over time. The inventory accounting policy had 'written off' this material – hardcore – to nil, but the company was still having to finance the purchase of this hardcore – about $30m worth. We instigated a sale process of the hardcore and released about $10m in working capital in the process – which was used to pay creditors, free up storage space and reduce administration. Be careful though with hardcore or obsolete stock disposal. There is a danger of diluting or damaging a product range or brand. Be careful who and how you sell to too – you do not want to turn stock into an uncollectable debt, and selling on a sale-or-return basis gives upside to the buyer and potential downside to the seller and possibly no improvement to the cash situation.

At Client A we also established a team that met first thing each morning to discuss inventory purchases and creditor payments. This small team would decide how best to employ the limited cash each day – which creditors should be paid first, which purchases could be delayed, if the expenditure was a like, or a want, or a need, which suppliers would get a phone call to negotiate better payment terms overall or on a particular order, and who internally they needed to have a discussion with to modify their behaviour with regards to expenditure.

Another useful ratio is Inventory Turnover, which measures how often the business replaces inventory relative to the cost of sales. The calculation is:

$$\text{Inventory Turnover} = \text{(Cost of goods sold)} \div \text{(Average value of inventory)}$$

The higher the ratio, usually, the better. Low turnover may indicate weak sales or too much inventory. Weak sales result in lower amounts of cash coming into the business. High inventory levels indicate too much cash tied up in inventory that could be better utilised in the business.

It should also be noted that Inventory Turnover needs to be reviewed more holistically than some other financial ratios. In some circumstances a high inventory turnover ratio can indicate a problem; for example, the business does not have enough inventory to support its strong sales. In times of high inflation or supply chain disruption – for example, the COVID-19 pandemic and during the Russia–Ukraine war – having high inventory levels can be an advantage to protect against price increases and increased demand. This was evident in Australia in the construction sector. Wood and other construction materials were in short supply and, along with labour shortages, resulted in delays in the time to build houses. Businesses then faced a cash crunch with higher material costs, higher labour costs, and a longer cash-to-cash cycle. During this time, I was talking to a client and she mentioned her new house was about to get started. I asked if she had asked the builder about certainty of materials and labour, and if the contract was fixed. She hadn't, but she did say the builder had been purchasing materials for her house since the day the contract was signed several months prior.

In some businesses it is easier to calculate an Inventory-to-Sales Ratio. This was the case at Client A.

Inventory-to-Sales Ratio = Sales
÷ (Average value of inventory)

At Client A, the number of stock line items and the amount of hardcore resulted in an Inventory-to-Sales Ratio of 2. The lower the number, the higher amount of investment in inventory to support the sales.

Inventory ratios should, like Debtor Days and Creditor Days, be benchmarked against the industry average. You would expect fashion retail businesses to have a higher inventory ratio than a manufacturing business, for example.

Expenditure management

This is usually what clients and their staff are most fearful of in a turnaround: a team of turnaround advisors coming into the business and slashing costs.

Expenditure is divided into:

- capital expenditure – for example, plant and equipment
- discretionary expenditure – for example, marketing, training, sponsorship
- non-discretionary expenditure – for example, wages and salaries, rent.

All expenditure is analysed and, where possible, at least initially capital and discretionary expenditure is halted until this analysis is completed. Where possible, capital projects will be renegotiated with more favourable terms. Discretionary expenditure may be discontinued, especially if the opportunity cost is less than the actual cost.

Though expenditure management is essential in a turnaround, unfortunately the benefits usually do not have an immediate impact on short-term cash management. For example, a reduction in staff, and therefore wages and salaries, is usually accompanied by redundancy costs, and actually makes the short-term cash position worse. Negotiating better terms for purchasing takes time, and there is often a transition period from an old supplier to a new one, and amounts owing to the old supplier that need payment.

Short-term financial support

After assessing the above cash-generation initiatives there still may not be enough cash to successfully execute a turnaround or for the business to survive long enough to do so. Extra cash may be required from an external source. The first support financiers are the two that are most familiar with the business: the bank and the shareholders/owner.

Approaching the bank needs to be navigated carefully. The bank (along with the Tax Office) is usually the largest creditor, and their support is needed, and at the same time you do not want to add further angst that would lead them to pull their funding and support.

In-person meetings are imperative when seeking financial support. The business owner or the CEO and Chair as well as the turnaround manager should be at such meetings. From the bank, aim to have the relationship manager, their manager, and importantly a risk team representative. Why? So the messages being conveyed by both the business and the bank are going directly to the decision-makers – there is nothing lost in translation. Also, for a successful outcome for both parties, a congenial relationship needs to be established and trust formed.

At Client A, they had around $100m in hedging contracts, and they were out-of-the-money (had lost money on the contracts). The bank's market relationship dealers visited Client A when I started and were about to call in the $1m that Client A owed. Now in a past life I was a currency trader at a large bank. Being able to talk to these bankers in their language, create a rapport and show them my credentials resulted in Client A being granted six weeks to get the hedging contracts 'in order' (a position where they were not losing money). A small win, but the hard work had just begun as the success of this, and the ongoing relationship, depended on following through and doing what we said we would do. Within the six weeks we did manage to get the hedging contracts in order, but the biggest win was the relationship that was established.

An advantage of an experienced turnaround manager is they may have existing relationships with the bank or will have experience negotiating with banks. They will add credibility to the negotiations. Likewise for the bank, having an experienced turnaround manager attend meetings increases their confidence in the turnaround.

When negotiating short-term financial support, keep in mind both the current lending agreement and the impacts of amending it. Often lending agreements have covenants linked to financial metrics and operating performance. These covenants are like traffic lights to funders; green all good, amber is watch and monitor, and red is stop funding. In my experience, Tier 1 trading banks are strict on the covenants, whereas Tier 2 lenders and collateral lenders are often more tolerant of broken covenants. All, however, require careful managing.

Banks will also be looking to improve their position. This may be in a number of forms: security, guarantees, interest cost. Adding further lending support is likely to worsen their position in the short term, so enter the negotiation understanding this, and also how your turnaround plan will improve their position. Be aware, though, that in improving the position for the bank, you may be worsening the position of other stakeholders – for example, shareholders or creditors – and you don't want to solve one problem but create another problem that may have worse implications.

Shareholders, family and creditors can be other sources of short-term financing support. The Australian Taxation Office is not (even though it is often referred to as the 'fifth bank'), and if you are relying on 'funding' from the ATO by not paying taxes and superannuation, you are in crisis, you're creating a bigger problem and you need to deal with it – today! Find a good turnaround manager!

Be wary of borrowing money from friends and family. Why?

- **Borrowing money from family and friends makes you lazy.**
  Don't you just love the Bank of Mum and Dad? There's not
  much, if any, paperwork, and they lend on very favourable terms.

Borrowing money from rich (or richer than you) benefactors makes you not think about ways to create and make money or fix the problems that created a cash squeeze. But to quote Dale Beaumont of Business Blueprint fame: 'If you can't make money without money, you'll never make money with money.' Dale's view is that borrowing money makes you lazy in business. He is talking about business startups, but borrowing money from family and friends when your business is in distress does not help address reasons for the financial woes or create an environment where you must be as accountable, say, as to a bank.

- **Raising finance from family and friends takes time and energy.** Raising capital (from any source) takes time and energy, and that is time and energy you should or could be spending on the business.

- **Borrowing money or raising capital from family and friends reduces your freedom.** You can say goodbye to autonomy! There may be strings attached to the funding. Some lenders will demand not only a return on the money, but also input into the related decision-making. To make decisions, people need information. So, several times a year, at least, you will have to provide these 'investors' with reports, plans and other information for them to provide informed input into your business. They will also expect their ideas to be implemented, and if they are not, you will need to explain why. Being indebted slows down decision-making, and for businesses in financial distress this is the time they need to be agile.

You will become accountable to stakeholders who know you well and interact with you on a personal level, not only for the monies that they lent you but for how you use that funding and what else you do with your time and resources. Often people start a business to gain a level of freedom – just think of all the so-called

'Mumpreneurs' or the semi-retired who want the flexibility to look after the grandchildren or play golf on Wednesdays, or the social media bloggers who like travelling. If I were to provide capital to your business, how happy do you think I would be if you told me you were going on holiday for three months or that you had just bought a new car?

- **It could cost you your reputation.** 'Your reputation is like a shadow, following you wherever you go,' said author and small business expert Frank Sonnenberg. If your business fails and you cannot return the capital you've borrowed, you lose your reputation as well as your money. If the investors are your family or mates, you could lose those relationships too.

- **You have to pay it back.** It is unlikely that family and friends, no matter how much they love you, will not require their money back. So even while you plan to use the funds to stabilise and then grow the business, these plans are now impacted by payments of interest, dividends and capital.

❛ If your business fails and you cannot return the capital you've borrowed, you lose your reputation as well as your money.

There is a time and a place for capital investment by family and friends, but this is usually when the business is mature and stable, and even then, it must be done with a strategic vision and planning.

Cash controls

The third step of turnaround cash management is cash control; that is, creating a tight system for day-to-day control of the cash. For SMEs it is usually relatively simple and in a centralised area or person, but in larger businesses and businesses across wider geographies and/or with multiple banking facilities this is more difficult, but having a centralised point of control is still important.[23]

In a turnaround context, and at least initially, the control of the cash needs to be tightened. First, the access and remittance of funds controls need to be reviewed. Who has access, and what limits, processes and controls are in place for spending money? The review will look at, and usually end up tightening, the following areas:

- **Authorisation access and limits.** Often over time people are added and/or limits are increased for payment authorisations.

- **Banking arrangements.** Over time there may be bank accounts and/or credit cards added.

- **Automatic payments.** These payments need to be reconsidered as part of the cashflow forecast and cash-generation initiatives.

Cash rationing

Cash rationing is a process to decide how to allocate cash to different areas or projects of the business, given the limited amount of cash available. The term 'cash rationing' is usually associated with larger and multi-site businesses where the cash control is brought back to a central point or site. However, in small businesses cash rationing can be achieved through bringing the decision-making back to a single person.

Effective cash rationing begins with a short-term forecast of expected cash movements in and out of the business. It may start with a weekly forecast over the next month and be reviewed weekly. There is a time lag, so for example if week 1 receipts were less than forecast there will be a reduction in cash expenditure of that amount

---

23 Large organisations often have a treasury team that manages the liquidity and funding and is the central point of cash control.

in week 2, and also the receipts forecast may need to be altered. In severe cases of limited cash, this process might be done daily rather than weekly.

Cash rationing is a retrospective and reactive control system, required because of actions and inactions that have occurred over time. It is a blunt tool to quickly change behaviours.

Chapter 5
Financial control

'A goal without a plan is just a wish.'

Antoine de Saint-Exupéry

Most small businesses – and the majority of medium-sized businesses – do not have a plan of any sort. If they do it is a financial plan 'because the bank needed one'. But this has long since been filed in the bottom drawer and has never been reviewed.

So, if most small and medium-sized businesses don't have plans, why should you have a plan for your business?

Let me ask this question: why do most large businesses have plans?

Large businesses have plans not just to keep bankers and investors happy – they have them as tools to better manage their business. They regard plans as a very powerful tool. That's why all businesses should have plans – to assist them to better manage their operations. Even the Australian Government's website business.gov.au outlines planning as the first step in starting a new business. When you register for an Australian Business Number, the ATO may call you and ask if you have a plan. They may even ask for a business plan if you have losses over consecutive years.

As Benjamin Franklin said, 'If you fail to plan, you are planning to fail.'

Developing plans is not easy. For most small business owners, their preference is to look at the detail and not the big picture – they are a practitioner and not a leader in the business, remember? I think the main reason they don't develop and follow a plan is because they are afraid of failure. 'What would happen if I had a big, hairy, audacious goal and didn't reach it? What would people think?'

When I'm working with business owners, I assure them that the goals of their business are *their* goals, and no-one else cares if they achieve their goals or not. I've never had a client ask me what *my* goals are, and I don't expect I ever will – they just don't care about my goals. Not setting a goal or plan is like turning up at the airport without a ticket and not knowing the destination. I ask them, 'What will you do?', and, 'How will you do it, and with whom?', and, 'What do you want out of the trip?'

> ❝ Not setting a goal or plan is like turning up at the airport without a ticket and not knowing the destination.

A goal or plan will set in place where your business is heading.

Then I assure them that they are more likely to get close to their goal if they set a plan. Remember when you were saving up for a car or a house deposit? I bet you had regular savings goals and stuck to a budget. In knowing how much you needed to put away each week or month, you were more likely to achieve or get close to achieving your goal than if you had no plan at all.

Zero-based budgeting

Along with the cashflow forecast, we can look at the whole business and develop a 'zero-based budget'.

Zero-based budgeting or ZBB has been around since the 1970s and was developed by Pete Pyhrr, a former accounting manager with Texas Instruments. The original goal of zero-based budgeting was to help businesses reduce costs and promote fiscal responsibility. It's a technique where a budget is formed with no regard to previous budgets or performance. It starts from a zero base – from scratch – and is not based on previous trends. By starting a budget from a zero base, you are forced to look at every single item in the budget, challenge and test the assumptions of each item, and decide what to include and exclude. Funds are then allocated based on justified need (and not likes or wants), leading to smarter spending.

Zero-based budgeting is different from expenditure management, however. Expenditure management is tactical, reactive, and often has a one-time decision. It focuses solely on costs and does not look at the medium or long-term consequences. Zero-based budgeting is proactive and considers both costs and income, is repeatable and focuses on accountability. In a turnaround situation it's about developing a plan where every dollar spent will deliver a positive return, and it is well understood why each dollar is being spent and what the expected output or return is for that dollar.

Zero-based budgeting is not easy to implement and is often time consuming. To implement zero-based budgeting, follow these steps:

1. When building the budget, you are starting from scratch and re-envisioning the business, and asking what activities and resources are needed in the future for this re-envisioned business. It is a vision but not a fairy tale – set a clear outlook with realistic costs.

2. Put together a comprehensive list of expenses. This needs to be very granular and not just a summary; for example, you could have a wide range of expenses summarised together as office expenses, but with zero-based budgeting you need a breakdown of all items and costs that make up office expenses.

3. Now that you have a granular list of current expenses, 'repackage' them into meaningful cost packages and subpackages; for example, business administration package, cost of goods sold package.

4. Develop price and consumption drivers – quality, consistency, quantity, reliability – for each package.

5. Assign owners to each package and empower the owners to generate initiatives for their packages in conjunction with the relevant business units.

6. Ensure package owners and business unit budget owners work together to develop a budget.

7. Ensure costs can be tracked and monitored (actual vs budget).

8. Have tools to make the budgeting and the monitoring process easy.

Though difficult to implement, and especially so for people who have not done so before, zero-based budgeting does deliver some real benefits for a business and especially so for a business in the midst of a turnaround:

- It allows for better alignment of expenditure and resources with the overall mission.
- It ensures key strategic imperatives are funded and removes costs that are not required (the wants and likes). Embedding of existing spend in the cost base is prevented.

- The conventional thinking and allocation of resources is addressed head on with all cost items challenged – even the ones with 'protected interests'. It eliminates common 'sandbagging' practices in the budgeting process.

- It creates transparency, as every cost is understood and the reason for the spend is also understood. It requires a detailed knowledge of departmental activities and a willingness to discontinue activities, and can reduce the 'we've always done that' factor.

- Fiscal management and investment decisions are more robust and therefore of better quality. It replaces 'do more with less' with 'do the right things with the right amount'.

- Zero-based budgeting can help lower costs by avoiding blanket increases or decreases to a prior period's budget.

3-statement forecast

Another budgeting and planning technique often used is a '3-statement forecast'. A 3-statement forecast uses three different financial reports:

- the balance sheet, which outlines what the business owns and what it owes

- the profit and loss statement, which outlines what a business receives and spends

- the cashflow statement or cashflow forecast (in distressed businesses I prefer the cashflow forecast), which shows where cash is being spent and how the business is being funded.

The 3-statement forecast integrates the three component statements in a dynamic way so the user can see the impact of decisions and scenarios; for example, if sales were to go up 2% you could see the impact on accounts receivable, debt, gross profit, overdrafts and so on, all at once. It is an extremely powerful tool to quickly see the impact of various situations in a turnaround.

A further benefit is that it's becoming common for banks to request a 3-statement forecast before considering funding applications.

A 3-statement forecast is usually done in an Excel spreadsheet, though accounting software is now starting to provide 3-statement forecasts in their reporting suites. I prefer an Excel spreadsheet as you can tailor it to your business needs and create the analysis for your specific requirements and not have the generic analysis from the accounting software. However, this also requires a bit of accounting and Excel skill to do well.

Chapter 6

Stakeholder management

'Stakeholders' is a broad term for any individual or group that has an interest or significant influence in the turnaround – both during the process and in the outcome. Stakeholders may include customers, creditors, financiers, employees, suppliers, subcontractors, regulators and the local community.

The aim of stakeholder management is to rebuild stakeholder confidence. By the time a turnaround has commenced, often stakeholder relationships have deteriorated to such an extent they have become adversarial. The turnaround leaders need to mend these relationships, and this will require them to:

- **Clearly articulate the overall plan.** This includes outlining milestones and timeframes, as well as the approach that will be taken.

- **Dissipate and overcome hostility towards the business or the key people in the business.** People need to be more than heard – they need to be listened to and feel their concerns are not being ignored.

- **Do what they say when they say they'll do it.** This builds credibility and trust.
- **Build a 'no surprises' culture.** People I have worked with will chuckle when they read this as it is extremely important to me – maybe the control freak in me. However, you can only manage and be accountable for what you can control. Surprises also create doubts – what other skeletons are in the cupboard, what other surprises are there, what else have I not been told? Doubts weaken trust and credibility.

Stakeholder support is imperative to the success of a turnaround. They are either going to be supporters or blockers, and obviously it is better for them to be supporters. The first step to rebuild the relationships is to identify the stakeholders, then analyse them to determine a priority or their importance, put in place a strategy to communicate with them, and align your interests and theirs.

Stakeholder identification

You might think you know who all the stakeholders are, but you do not want to inadvertently miss including a stakeholder, so get organised. This applies to small sole trader turnarounds through to large publicly listed corporates.

Start with a brainstorming session and think who is affected by your business and the work you do. Who has some influence or power over your business or you? Who has an interest in the success, or failure, of the turnaround? Use a whiteboard and put the following stakeholder group headings and subheadings.

Stakeholder group	Stakeholder sub-group
Internal stakeholders	• Your boss • Board • Shareholders • Employees
Your family	• Shareholders • Immediate family • Key supporters (may be friends, local community, businesses nearby)
Creditors, suppliers and financiers	• Banks • Suppliers • Creditors • Bank of Mum and Dad • Tax Office
Customers	• Key customers • Future or prospective customers
Regulators	• Bankruptcy or insolvency regulators • Corporate regulators • Unions • Licencing authorities • Industry associations • Leave and superannuation authorities[24]
Advisors	• Accountants • Lawyers • Recruitment advisors • PR and marketing advisors

You can see there are many stakeholders – probably more than you first imagined. Stakeholders are both individuals and groups, so where there are individuals, identify all those individuals.

---

24 Long-service leave, portable long-service leave, and superannuation authorities and schemes are common in some industries; for example, construction and community services.

Prioritise stakeholders

Different stakeholders will have different levels of influence and different levels of interest in your business and the turnaround. For the turnaround, we need to be clear where each stakeholder or stakeholder group sits in the power and interest matrix. The position on the matrix below indicates the actions and effort required to manage them.

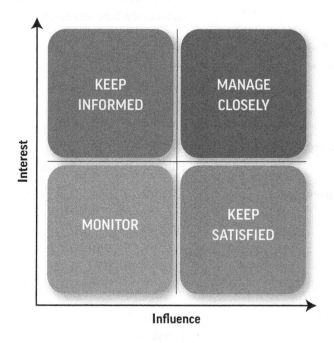

- **Monitor:** These stakeholders have little influence and low interest in the turnaround. While all stakeholders are important, the communication and engagement level can be low here.
- **Keep informed:** These stakeholders need more information and perhaps direct engagement (talk to them). They may be useful with helping with the detail of the project. An example may be the parent and former owner of the business.

- **Keep satisfied:** Put enough effort to keep these stakeholders engaged and satisfied, but there is a balance to not swamp them with information.
- **Manage closely:** This group of stakeholders need full engagement and the greatest effort.

Your major funder may fall into the 'manage closely' quadrant, family members might be in the 'keep informed' quadrant, the neighbouring businesses might be in the 'monitor' quadrant and major customers may be in the 'keep satisfied' quadrant.

You then need to understand your stakeholders and how they feel about the turnaround. Some questions to ask yourself (or the stakeholders directly if there are not too many):

- What is their level of interest in the turnaround outcome – both financially and emotionally?
- What information do they require and how do they like to be communicated with?
- What is their opinion of you, your products or services, and your business?
- What motivates them?
- Who influences their opinions and decisions? Should a stakeholder's influencer be added as your stakeholder?
- If they are not a supporter, what would change them to a supporter?
- If they are not a supporter and are unlikely to ever become one, how will you manage their opposition?

After answering these questions, put each stakeholder on the matrix and then colour code them, with green being a supporter, neutral stakeholders in amber and critics and blocker stakeholders in red.

At the end of this exercise, you will be quite clear on how each stakeholder needs to be managed, and then you can put together a communication plan.

Stakeholder communication

Communication is an essential part of the turnaround process. In the Emergency phase there is a lot of activity, uncertainty, ideas and thoughts.

Using our medical analogy, it's like what you expect when a patient is brought into an emergency room – doctors and nurses hurrying about trying to assess and keep alive the patient. Meanwhile, in the waiting room family and friends, and possibly the police, congregate. They talk among themselves with their worries, hypotheses, anecdotes, speculation, and the police are conducting interviews and monitoring the situation.

In the business turnaround the family and friends are the employees, suppliers, customers, shareholders and creditors, and the police may be regulators, or legal or insolvency teams for some of the stakeholders. All are thirsty for information and want to know three things:

- How bad is the current state of affairs?
- What is being done to stop things getting worse?
- What is the plan to make things better?

The turnaround leader needs to provide this information and some guidance.

Lack of communication is also a cause of business distress, and can heighten levels of angst. If you feel overwhelmed, exhausted and stop communicating with your stakeholders, uncertainty, mistrust and doubt will grow.

The turnaround leader needs to develop a communication strategy that covers what to communicate, when to communicate and how to communicate.

What to communicate

- **Essential information only:** You want the message to get through, and not get lost in the noise of other, perhaps interesting but not necessary, information.
- **The turnaround vision:** All stakeholders are invested in some way in the turnaround. Share the high-level vision of the turnaround strategy, including financial goals and how they will be met.
- **Share both what you know and what you don't:** People appreciate honesty, and it builds credibility. Share both the good news and the bad news too. Do not feel you must have all the answers, and acknowledge the situation is 'fluid'.
- **Embrace brevity:** Do not write a three-page memo padding out a key message that could be explained in one paragraph.
- **Consistent messages:** Do not tell one group of stakeholders – for example, employees – one message and another group of stakeholders – for example, shareholders – another message. A consistent story is a believable story.

When to communicate

- **Don't keep shtum:** Silence is not golden in a turnaround. Silence creates anxiousness, worry, misinformation and distrust. People do not like surprises, and rumours erode confidence. Communicate openly and frequently.
- **Anticipate questions:** In times of crisis, people are overwhelmed and may not have the capacity to think of all the questions they

would like answers to. Anticipate this and have answers to questions they may have down the track. For example, you may need to tell staff there will be redundancies, so have information around their entitlements and even the Australian Government Fair Entitlements Guarantee.[25]

- **Share with others after you have taken care of yourself:** Sounds selfish, but if the turnaround leader does not take care of themself, they are not in a good place to lead others.

How to communicate

- **Embrace various mediums of communication:** Different people have different preferences for how they like to receive information. My kids don't read emails or make phone calls; they get their information via messages – texts, Messenger, Snapchat and the like. My wife is deaf, so her preferred medium is email or text messages. Me – I prefer a phone call. In a turnaround I prefer face-to-face communication – it humanises the situation and builds a relationship and trust.

- **Eyeball to eyeball:** There is a qualitative difference in the ability to read emotions and connect on a personal level when we communicate in person.

- **Two-way communication:** Give an opportunity for stakeholders to provide responses, and listen to ensure you understand. The turnaround leader's role is not always to solve each stakeholders' problem but sometimes to just sit and listen. If stakeholders really feel heard, they will be more engaged in the turnaround. Be prepared to accept negative emotions and conflict (within reason). Different people deal with a crisis differently so be patient and graceful.

---

25 The Fair Entitlements Guarantee is a scheme of last resort that provides financial assistance for unpaid employee entitlements in insolvency.

- **With care:** Prepare to communicate with stakeholders and plan the message you want to deliver. What you say and how you say it will either increase confidence or crush it – do not put your foot in your mouth.

- **Manage conflicts and challenges:** Conflicts will occur and should be anticipated and managed. Do so in a respectful and timely manner. There does not need to be 'us' and them' or 'winners' and 'losers'. Be constructive and aim for a 'win–win' situation.

- **Leverage support:** The turnaround leader is not an 'island'. Key stakeholders can provide support and influence to help overcome barriers and 'grease wheels'.

Part III

CRISIS STABILISATION PHASE

The prior phase – the Emergency phase of business triage – is all about doing what is necessary for the business to survive. It has 'bought' some time to allow stabilisation of the business and to move forward making some necessary structural changes. The Crisis Stabilisation phase is about moving the business to operating as a normal, functional business.

I have discussed how in a living being the brain and the heart are the most vital organs and the blood vessels that link them are required to ensure they keep operating. In the Emergency phase the patient – the business – had a heart attack, and the focus was on getting the heart and brain working and the blood (cash) moving.[26] In the Emergency phase the actions were business CPR.[27] After a person has a heart attack and is resuscitated, the doctors put in place strategies to prevent further heart attacks such as living a healthy lifestyle, managing other medical conditions, and taking medicine as directed. It is now about focusing on moving forward in a healthy, sustainable way and on building the new. Health is wealth! Also, like recovering from a heart attack and making sustainable lifestyle changes, hard work is required. Sanjiv Kapoor, former Chief Operating Officer of SpiceJet who is attributed with the successful turnaround of the airline in 2014, which was described as a 'miracle', said, 'There is no such thing as a miracle turnaround. There's a lot of hard work, lot of hard work and planning, and real perseverance.'

---

26 A heart attack occurs when the flow of blood to the heart is severely reduced or blocked.
27 Cardiopulmonary resuscitation.

Too often businesses and business owners think that once the initial crisis is averted, they are over the immediate threat of ceasing operations and the turnaround is over. 'We're good to take it from here.' But the Crisis Stabilisation phase is the longest phase of the turnaround process and can take a couple of years.

> 'There is no such thing as a miracle turnaround. There's a lot of hard work, lot of hard work and planning, and real perseverance.'

In this stage we address the internal issues of the business by addressing leadership, strategic focus, organisational change, process improvement and financial restructuring.

Chapter 7

Leadership

Leadership is a set of behaviours used to help people align their collective direction, to execute strategic plans, and to continually renew a business.[28] Effective leaders also understand that every situation is different and what works in one situation may not work every time. During a crisis the role of leaders and the impact of their decisions and actions are amplified. In addition, the shock or realisation of the consequences of the crisis can paralyse leaders. Therefore, leadership and leadership strategy must adapt to the context and stage of the business turnaround.

Situational leadership

There are many theoretical leadership styles; for example, transformational leadership, transactional leadership, charismatic leadership, supervisory leadership, cognitive leadership and directive leadership. However, each of these have their limitations and

---

28 McKinsey & Company, 2022.

issues in crisis management. Therefore, a combination of different leadership styles is needed, and effective leaders should be able to demonstrate multiple leadership competencies and styles as an ensemble. This is known as 'situational leadership'.

Situational leadership encourages leaders to weigh the many variables in their business, consider the team members they have, and choose the leadership style that best fits each situation or circumstance. Situational leaders move from one leadership style to another or demonstrate multiple leadership styles simultaneously to meet the changing needs of the business and the employees. During a business crisis, employees are likely to demonstrate different levels of readiness to handle the situation. Situational leaders choose the appropriate leadership style to match with the staff's level of readiness to enhance their productivity and competitiveness. Situational leaders, therefore, must demonstrate a high level of different leadership competencies during the crisis.

There are seven broad benefits of situational leadership:

- **It increases awareness of the current business situation.**
  When a business is in distress and undertaking a turnaround,
  the change is unsettling, and staff may have real concerns about
  their tenure and also their roles or functions. The situational
  leadership approach can help ease any fear of the staff regarding
  their job security. The situational leadership approach is a
  people-oriented leadership style and situational leaders are
  honest and transparent with their teams. If you get employees to
  buy in to your business aspirations, the journey towards the goal
  will be a lot faster, smoother and more successful.

- **Situational leaders can counter volatility** by leading their
  team to concentrate on their work responsibilities and not on the
  political matters. They can adjust to the situation by exercising a
  task-oriented leadership approach and keeping their employees

on the right track of achieving the business goals, despite
different political belief systems that might be present.

- **Situational leaders can counter uncertainty** that can result
  in a decrease in productivity, tension between co-workers,
  and possibly an unstable business too. A successful situational
  leader will shift into a charismatic leader in times like these.
  They must know how to show empathy to individuals while
  remaining rational rather than adding to the stress. They should
  understand how their employees' fear of uncertainty is affecting
  their job performance, so they can provide coaching and
  support accordingly. A good leader must have clarity of vision to
  influence their team to stay focused on the business goals.

- **Situational leaders can decipher situational complexity.** They
  can see from different perspectives and are able to simplify things.
  They can focus on the simpler things that really matter to solve
  complex issues. People will continue to be complex. The business
  environment of tomorrow will continue to be complicated. Solving
  the business distress issue is complex and takes time.

- **Situational leaders can beat ambiguity.** US Army War College
  developed a leadership concept called VUCA – volatility,
  uncertainty, complexity and ambiguity – after the 9/11 terrorist
  attacks. VUCA in a business turnaround is inescapable,
  however the situational leader can break VUCA down into its
  component parts, and identify volatile, uncertain, complex
  or ambiguous situations. Each type of situation has its own
  causes and resolutions, so you should aim to deal with one at
  a time. Counter volatility with vision, meet uncertainty with
  understanding and by listening, react to complexity with clarity
  and clear communication, and fight ambiguity with agility
  and the promotion of flexibility, and with people that thrive in
  VUCA environments.

- **Using situational leadership, you can control all possible outcomes** because you are able to effectively influence your business in all directions: upwards, across and down. You think proactively and consider how your subordinates will react. You formulate scenarios of how to handle every possible reaction. The situational leader is a good chess player. They are self-aware and therefore they use their leadership intuition and back it up with years of experience and academic training. A situational leadership approach allows the leader to look beyond what others see in plain sight.

- **Situational leaders adapt their style to those they lead.** A successful situational leader understands the importance of being charismatic at specific times. When they are trying to sell an idea that they perceive to be a bit more unconventional which may face resistance from superiors, peers or subordinates, they know how to switch on their charisma to gain their buy-in and cooperation. Situational leadership is adaptive, emotionally intelligent and influential. They know how to 'read the room'.

Attributes and characteristics of good turnaround leaders

The importance of strong leadership in a turnaround cannot be downplayed. Turnarounds are difficult, they are complex, they are time sensitive, they are chaotic. They are not for the faint-hearted, the tired or the passive. They are not for those that like managing from their office.

The leaders also need a passion for the turnaround, and must enjoy, thrive and perform well in difficult situations. They must believe they have a unique opportunity to make a meaningful difference, and be able to see the potential for the business and envision a successful turnaround. They also must be self-aware of their skills. At Byronvale Advisors we do not believe we have all the skills and knowledge for every business turnaround or engagement – but we know how to recognise the gaps and fill them with a bespoke team of the right people, in the right place, and at the right time. A turn-around leader does not necessarily have the right answers, but they should know the right questions to ask.

Well-known Australian director Ann Sherry AO[29], commenting on why business leaders are not coming forward to take on turnaround leadership roles, said, 'Most people are motivated to do the safest things with the highest rewards. Turnarounds rarely offer this.'[30]

Stephen Barnes – on the tools, shoulder deep and immersed in a turnaround.

---

29 Ann Sherry was CEO of Carnival Australia from 2016–19 and led their turnaround. She has also been CEO and director of a number of large corporates and not-for-profit organisations, and at the time of writing is Chancellor of Queensland University of Technology.
30 Vorbach & Pan, 2017.

Turnaround leaders like being shoulder deep in the business and the turnaround. They embed themselves in the business, attend meetings at all levels and get involved in the business. One of my first turnarounds was with a courier business, and I had a day in a van doing parcel collections in the morning, and then driving to a town three hours away stopping at every petrol station, post office and shop, before turning around and racing to the airport for a final drop off and returning the van. I had a whole day talking to the courier driver, and also some of the customers. This was an invaluable information-gathering and rapport-building exercise and, I believe, really helped with being able to lead the turnaround.

From a more functional perspective I find these characteristics essential for turnaround leaders:

- **A wide range of skills:** A good turnaround leader is a polymath – they have a wide range of skills, knowledge and/or experience in a number of subjects or areas. However, this does not mean having certain sector experience is a prerequisite for a turnaround leader (as discussed earlier). The business does not have a sector problem, they have a distressed business problem, a situational problem and a leadership problem.

- **Good spider senses:** It does (but shouldn't) surprise me when clients and their staff are surprised when I know when something is not quite right or what is actually happening at 'ground zero', just like a spider can sense rain. A good turnaround leader knows when something is off and when to keep digging.

- **Strong motivation:** The turnaround leader cannot achieve the turnaround on their own. They need to bring others along the journey, motivating and influencing them to get results. They also should be able to leverage relationships to increase effectiveness of the staff.

- **Problem-solving ability:** A good turnaround leader can take complex information and simplify the problem using conceptual and analytical thinking. They can then put new thinking to old problems. They should seek their own answers to questions. Failure to do so may inadvertently lead to the same situation that caused the problem in the first place.

- **Action oriented:** There is a requirement to make rapid, strategic decisions. There is not time to navel gaze and consider a long-term strategic plan. It's analogous to preparing for a bushfire and putting it out. Preventing bushfires takes time and proactivity. Fighting a bushfire, you need to be decisive, directive and immediate.

- **Result driven:** While turnaround leaders enact a turnaround plan, and plans and planning help identify problems and help formulate ways to mitigate them, the turnaround leader also needs to set clear expectations of staff and make them accountable. The good turnaround leader also demonstrates initiative and perseverance in executing a turnaround plan.

- **Authentic:** Look for a turnaround leader who wants to turn the business around, and not one that is there because it's their job, or they are interested in the fee alone. You want your turnaround leader to have your, and your business's, best interests at heart.

- **Confident:** The good turnaround leader is at least outwardly confident to lead, and displays confidence by staying focused and committed. Turnarounds are hard and there will be setbacks, but the work is important, and the turnaround leader needs to be confident and resolved.

- **Trustworthy:** Particularly at the start of a turnaround, trust is a rare commodity, with external stakeholders but also importantly with internal stakeholders such as the staff. A good turnaround leader earns trust and empowers staff. Usually, they do this by doing what they say they will do, when they say they will do it. Apart from developing trust it demonstrates accountability and sets expectations.

- **Ability to network:** Every turnaround is different and requires people with different skills, knowledge and experience. Because I'm old(er) I say I have a small team and a large Rolodex[31] – a large network. This network becomes my 'team'.

- **Ability to question:** Turnarounds are analogous to playing chess. Chess is a strategy game and the best players have figured out their moves half a dozen steps ahead of where they currently are. Good turnaround leaders do not rely on the moment, do not rely on answers at face value, and do their own investigations. For example, instead of asking the manager why there is a problem on the workshop floor, the turnaround leader may go down to the floor themselves, observe, and talk to the workers. Then they may ask the manager a question. Often the turnaround leader will have the answer before they ask the question. The question is not asked to establish the answer, but to provide context and validity.

---

31 A Rolodex is a rotating card file device used to store business contact information.

Chapter 8
Strategic focus

So far, we have focused on turnaround strategies to firstly enable the business to survive and then stabilise. This might have been over a period of just a few weeks or months, but the turnaround typically will take two to three years. The focus now transitions to the medium term and how to ensure stability and then growth of the business. We have 'bought' the time to now evaluate and be proactive in our turnaround strategy.

> *'The secret of change is to focus all your energy not on fighting the old, but on building the new.'*
>
> Socrates

Strategic plans

We've already looked at the importance of having a business plan. Plans help you stay organised and co-ordinate your efforts.

A plan is out of date almost as soon as it is written because things happen along the way that you can't prepare for. They can be good things, such as a new client coming on board or implementing a more efficient system that saves you time and money. Or they can be bad, such as adverse regulation changes, labour shortages, supply chain issues or rampant inflation.

Most plans do not build in slack to account for these unknowns. But the inaccuracy in plans does not make them worthless – in fact it is the process of planning that is most useful. Planning helps you understand the risks, dependencies and resourcing of your business. As Dwight D. Eisenhower said: 'No battle was ever won according to a plan, but no battle was won without one ... plans are useless, but planning is indispensable.'

Planning with strategy in mind

A strategic plan is the foundation or primary plan for your business and is essential for the turnaround to be successful. It is your roadmap for the medium term – approximately the next three to five years – and establishes where the business, via the turnaround process, is headed. It sets out the organisational vision, mission and values and focuses the energy, time and resources of the business in the same direction. It points to specific results that are to be achieved and establishes a course of action for achieving them. A strategic plan also helps the various divisions or sections within a business align themselves with common goals. Without a strategic plan, a business will wander aimlessly, and priorities will change constantly as the turnaround leader and stakeholders become confused about the turnaround process. Businesses that perform at the highest levels have a formalised strategic plan in place and implement it well. That is what we are aiming for with a business turnaround. Once you have developed your strategic plan, the key to making it work is to commit to seeing it through and implementing it across all areas of the business.

6 A strategic plan is the foundation or primary plan for your business and is essential for the turnaround to be successful.

The strategic planning process

Building a strategic plan is not difficult, and the process I undertake is the same as for a business that is not in distress. Think of the strategic planning process as being like planning an overseas family holiday. First, you'll need to know where you want to go and why. Then you can create the details of your trip, such as the length of time you will spend away, how much time you will be off work for, how much the airfares will cost and what activities you will do.

With a strategic plan, it's about defining your:

- mission
- values
- vision.

Let's consider each in turn, and I will show you how to design your strategic plan.

Mission statement

Your mission statement addresses the 'why we exist' question. It determines why you are in business and is a statement of your business's purpose. It focuses directly on the business you are presently in, and the customer needs you are presently striving to meet. It determines what is 'in' and what is 'out'.

The mission statement should serve as the foundation for everything you do – both for current day-to-day operations and as a foundation for future decision-making. It should also be concise. As Peter Drucker said, 'your mission should fit on a t-shirt'.

To give you an idea of what your mission statement should say, here are a few mission statements from well-known organisations:

- **Google:** 'To organize the world's information and make it universally accessible and useful.'
- **Warby Parker:** 'Warby Parker was founded with a rebellious spirit and lofty objective: to offer designer eyewear at a revolutionary price, while leading the way for socially conscious businesses.'
- **International Red Cross:** 'To provide relief to victims of disaster and help people prevent, prepare for and respond to emergencies.'

It is quite clear in these examples why these organisations exist.

Values statement

Next, consider your values. Values clarify what your business stands for and believes in, and the behaviours you expect to see from your employees and yourself as a result. They are the beliefs that guide the conduct, activities and goals of the business, and they establish what you do and what you stand for.

The values of a business form the cornerstone of its organisational culture and are to be upheld throughout your business. As such, when you are defining your business's values, it is important to get input from all staff. An anonymous survey will get the best response from your staff as values are personal, and people need to feel they can share their values without any influence or judgment. Having input from everyone involved in your business means the values statement has meaning and is not just a list of ideas that no-one is interested in.

Some questions that you might ask when considering your values are:

- What are the guiding principles for how you treat each other and your customers?

- What are the key non-negotiables that are critical to the success of the business?
- What are the guiding principles that are core to how you operate in this business?
- What behaviours do you expect to see?

The outcome is a values statement that articulates what your business believes in and a statement that holds true. It should comprise five to seven core and shared values. You may think that values are a given, but when they are articulated they can be used as a guide for reinforcement, training, rewards and consequences for poor behaviour and alignment of goals. It is not sufficient to determine your business's values and just post them on the business website – they need to be integrated into the day-to-day operations of the business. This way the values will come to life and become real.

Years ago, ANZ Bank implemented a hugely successful cultural change project called 'Breakout'. Starting at the top of the business and then moving down to the rank and file, staff went through a program that addressed their values and then the values of the bank. These values underpinned everything the bank did and were a guiding principle for training, staff remuneration and roles. The internal staff satisfaction levels soared as the cultural transformation occurred. The customer satisfaction also soared. Essentially what ANZ Bank did was address the four value-based questions above and then integrated them into the day-to-day operations of the bank.

Vision statement

Using the mission statement and the values statement, and the data you have gathered through the Analysis phase, you can now determine where you want to be – your business's goal and your vision for the business. Your vision statement answers the question, 'Where is the business going?' If it is not clear where the business is going, you cannot create a plan.

> 6 Your vision statement answers the question, 'Where is the business going?' If it is not clear where the business is going, you cannot create a plan.

Vision statements are aspirational big hairy audacious goals (BHAGs). Here are some well-known BHAGs from recognisable sources:

- **John F Kennedy:** 'We will put a man on the moon before the end of the decade and bring him back.'
- **Microsoft:** 'A computer on every desk and in every home using great software as an empowering tool.'
- **Amazon:** 'Our vision is to be earth's most customer centric company; to build a place where people can come to find and discover anything they might want to buy online.'

To come up with a strong vision statement, consider the following key elements:

- **Future casting.** The vision statement should provide a picture of what the future looks like for the business long term. It tries to envision your company's future.
- **Short and sweet.** The statement should be two sentences maximum. It is an elevator pitch but just between two floors.
- **Clear and visible.** You need to be able to see your business at its 'goal'. The words cannot be open to interpretation.
- **Audacious and ambitious.** The vision statement is a dream beyond what you currently think is possible.
- **Motivating.** It must inspire you, your staff and your customers.

- **Purpose driven.** It must give a reason or purpose for doing what you are doing.
- **Inspiring.** The language must be bold and engaging.
- **Capitalises on core competencies.** It must build on the business's current competencies.

Not all businesses get their vision statement right. Here are a couple of not-so-great vision statements:

> *'Build the best product, cause no unnecessary harm, use business to inspire and implement solutions to the environmental crisis.'*

> *'Provide maximum value for our shareholders whilst helping our customers to fulfil their dreams.'*

While the first vision is ambitious and even inspirational, I have no idea what 'best product', 'no unnecessary harm' and 'inspire and implement solutions' really mean.

The second example could apply to any company; it's not unique or inspiring. Who would know that this was an insurance company's vision statement?

It is important not to confuse mission and vision. A mission explains *why* you exist, your purpose. The vision explains *where* you are heading, your goal.

In the diagram below, 'A' is where the business is now. 'B' is your vision or goal.

The box is your mission. I call it a paddock, and the type of farm is determined by what is in the paddock. Make sure the only things your business does are within the paddock, or mission, and therefore also make sure your vision is within the paddock.

When it comes to creating your vision statement, you have a few options. It can be:

- **Quantitative.** It includes words to the effect of, 'to have 10,000 users of our software in ten years' time'.
- **Competitive.** You might be trying to outdo competitors and state something such as, 'to be the only provider of cloud-based accounting software in the SME market in Australia'.
- **Superlative.** Your vision is to be the most exceptional or outstanding, such as, 'the number one volume building company in Melbourne'.

To put a vision statement together, get as many of your staff on board as you can. The vision statement is not about delivering the vision to your staff but is about getting them engaged and buying into the vision.

Strategic objectives

Your mission, values and vision have to be supported by strategic objectives. Many businesses miss this step in their strategic planning.

Developing your objectives

Listing your objectives is the next step in developing your general, high-level methods or strategic objectives that you will use to reach your vision. Compiling this list will determine the most direct or clearest path from where you are now to where you want to be. In a turnaround process this is the milestones during that process.

Let's revisit the paddock diagram. Your objectives should set you on a straight course to get from A (your business now) to B (where you want to be).

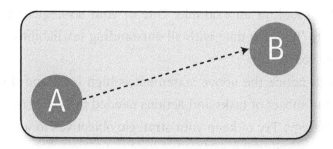

Start by articulating the turnaround strategy, and then put in place a set of manoeuvres or guardrails to keep you close to the straight or direct path to reach your business's goal or vision. This answers the 'how' question – how is your business going to reach its vision? The strategic objectives are high level, general statements that guide and cover a range or set of activities. They are used to operationalise the mission statement and help to provide guidance on how the business can fulfil or move towards its vision.

The strategic objectives, like the vision, are long term in nature. They should collectively address all areas of the business – finance, people, customers, marketing, sales, processes and operations.

❝ The strategic objectives, like the vision, are long term in nature. They should collectively address all areas of the business – finance, people, customers, marketing, sales, processes and operations.

A structure you may want to follow to develop your strategic objectives is:

Action + Detail + Metric + Unit + Deadline

Let's take a look at an example. One of your strategic objectives might be to 'be up to date with all outstanding tax liabilities in the next three years'.

You will notice the above statement is high level and does not address the subset of tasks and actions needed to deliver the objective or strategy. Try to keep your strategic objectives to a sentence that is easy to remember and understand.

Actions to achieve the strategic objectives

Your strategic objectives now need to be broken down into actions or tasks that can be converted into specific performance targets. They have to address what needs to be completed in the short term to achieve the strategic objectives.

To formulate actions, you may like to use the SMART principle:

- **Specific.** Answer the questions 'how much?' and 'what kind?' with each action.

- **Measurable.** Without being measurable, your objectives will lack accountability and will be just good intentions.

- **Attainable.** While an aspirational goal may inspire you, if the action is not attainable all you are doing is setting up for failure.

- **Responsible person.** Each action needs to have a champion to ensure the action is completed.

- **Time specific.** Set a realistic time when the action needs to be delivered.

Articulating your competitive advantage

All businesses need to know their competitive advantage to succeed. In other words, what is your business best at? If you do not have a clear idea of this, why will clients and customers use your products and services?

To establish your business's competitive advantage, you need to consider what the characteristics of your business are that allow it to meet your customers' needs better than your competition. It may take some time to narrow this down. To get started, you should use this simple formula:

Business name + Best at + Why

For example: Joe's Plumbing + Residential plumbing services + On time, courteous service. Once you know what your competitive advantage is, it needs to be built into your strategic plan. Being able to articulate your competitive advantage is a vital step in your turn-around planning process, and it is one that is often missed.

Measuring success and reviewing your plan

The final part of the process is to put in place a system for measuring success. These are often called key performance indicators (KPIs), and they are vital for ensuring the actions that will move your business through the strategic plan to the vision are on track – hopefully along that straight line.

It is important to use quantifiable measures. These will ensure accountability. They serve to make sure the actions are aligned, or realigned, to the tasks and strategic objectives.

Strategic planning is not a case of 'set and forget'. A review of your strategic plan is often thought of as something you do down the track when you have implemented the turnaround plan. This is partly true. However, it should also be incorporated into the building phase.

Remember that the strategic plan outlines how you are going to move from the present status to where you want to be – your vision.

> ❝ Remember that the strategic plan outlines how you are going to move from the present status to where you want to be – your vision.

It is vital that during the journey there are regular reviews of the strategic plan to ensure it is still relevant and that the actions undertaken are not deviating from the mission and the strategic objectives to attain the vision.

Strategic plans are guidelines and not rules. Ask the following types of questions when you review your strategic plan:

- Will your goals be achieved in the timeframes in the plan? If not, why not?
- Should the timeframes and deadlines be modified? Why should they be modified?
- Are the goals and actions still realistic and relevant? Should they be changed?
- Should there be a change in focus to put more emphasis on achieving the goals, or a particular goal?

The point is to reaffirm the mission and vision, and then ensure you are not diverting from the straight line between the two. The objectives are part of the plan – without them you only have a mission, value and vision statement.

Strategic turnaround plan execution

Your strategic turnaround plan is more than a piece of paper. It is not a tick-the-box exercise for stakeholders – it has to be much more than that.

Executing your strategic turnaround plan is as important, if not more important, than developing your strategy. It moves it from a document that sits in the bottom drawer to actions that drive organisational change and growth. You need it. The business needs it. Your stakeholders need it. It builds credibility and trust and instils confidence.

Implementation of your plan addresses the who, where, when and how, whereas the strategy addresses the what and why.

You need to review and track the goals and objectives you have set for your business, otherwise your plan will be regarded as a one-off exercise rather than something that is ongoing. The plan is not to be only discussed annually at a 'weekend retreat'. It is to be communicated regularly and widely with all stakeholders. Unless everyone is told about it, how can you expect them to understand it and contribute to it? Lack of ownership of the plan is a big risk. If people do not take responsibility for the plan, it will continue to be business as usual.

Another risk to the successful implementation of your plan is that it is regarded as the 'Oh my God' plan – it's too large, too grand, and the goals and actions required to implement it are too numerous and it is difficult to prioritise which steps to take first. This is where having an experienced turnaround advisor will help – they have been there, done that. By not considering the plan's implementation, creating the plan is seen as an end in itself, and how it is going to be implemented is not discussed during the planning process.

Avoiding the planning pitfalls

One of the challenges with implementing your plan is that it can be hard to track progress. Sure, you can ask for progress reports, but often it's tempting just to measure what is easy and not what is important. When this happens, momentum stalls and everyone becomes frustrated.

To get around this, make sure you ask people in your business to be accountable. With accountability comes empowerment. If they are going to be made responsible for helping to successfully implement the plan, you need to give them the authority and the tools necessary to impact the relevant measures.

Hold an annual review

Despite having warned you of only reviewing your plan once a year, it is important that, as well as the regular reviews, you do hold an annual strategic review and provide all stakeholders with an annual update.

Do not invite everyone to this update. Too many people create 'management by committee', which is not conducive to well-thought-out decision-making and strong leadership. However, you might want to consider having a cross-section of your employees attend.

Other tips for holding a successful annual strategy update are:

- **Address the 'elephant in the room'.** This should be done prior to the annual update. Don't let the 'elephant' disrupt the annual update and become the focus of the session.
- **Do your homework.** Come armed with facts and don't waste time during the update conducting research on the go.
- **Use a facilitator.** This is crucial. A good facilitator will keep the meeting on track and keep the process moving towards the desired outcome. I have never seen a good strategic day without a facilitator. This may be your turnaround advisor.
- **Focus on the outcomes and not the agenda.** While getting through the agenda is what it usually takes to get a completed plan, focusing on outcomes is more important.
- **Explain the process.** The facilitator should explain the process so that everyone is on the same page, and no-one is left behind.

When this happens, the meeting can focus on outcomes and not become side-tracked or derailed.

- **Don't assume everyone thinks like you.** Walk in other people's shoes. Not everyone has the same preferences as you. Also, no matter how hard you try, you cannot change people's preferences. Learn to work with those preferences rather than trying to change them.

- **Don't overlook life after the meeting.** Going back to business as usual, as if you never had a strategic planning meeting, is a waste of everyone's time and money, and makes it virtually impossible to get participation and engagement in the future. Don't let this happen!

Chapter 9
Organisational change

The Greek philosopher Heraclitus said, 'the only constant in life is change', and one of the ways businesses become distressed or fail is through lack of change – boiled frogs.

> ❝ The Greek philosopher Heraclitus said, 'the only constant in life is change'.

Organisational change is the process of moving from established to new ways of thinking, behaving or working. It can cause major shifts in the structure, culture, goals, operational processes, service offerings and technology policies of a business. As a distressed business needs to change what it has and is doing, all business turn-arounds require organisational change. To quote Winston Churchill, 'to improve is to change'.

Organisational change, however, takes time – it does not occur immediately in the turnaround process. It usually happens after the review of the strategic focus and therefore is part of the Crisis Stabilisation phase of the turnaround triage model.

There are four areas of organisational change: structure, personnel, capabilities and employment rewards and conditions. Combined these will bring about a change in culture and a new way of doing things.

Structure change

Organisational structural change is a change in organisational hierarchy, chain of command, management systems, job structure or administrative procedures. A merger is the most common cause of a structural change in a business.

Structural change occurs after strategic change. It is premature to change the structure of the business until the 'Point B' – where the business is heading, the vision, the 'paddock', the mission, what the business does, and the route and how it is going to get there – are established. In other words, the strategy. The strategic plan provides clarity on the intended result of the change. During this strategic planning process many of the structural problems will be identified.

Structural change is analogous to building a house. The architect spends time with the clients, the builders, the council and the developers, understanding the requirements of each stakeholder. Good design requires an in-depth understanding, time and effort. To reiterate, it should not be part of the Emergency phase of the turnaround and should be after the strategic focus has been established. However, for every rule there can be exceptions – such as to establish management control, and the requirements of cost or asset reductions needs. These might be done as part of the Emergency phase.

Flattening the structure

Underperforming businesses are often operated in a pyramid structure, with the workers on the bottom and then various levels of seniority above to the CEO. However, in the Crisis Stabilisation phase the organisational structure needs to be realigned so the vitality of the turnaround process is preserved and the disorder and its corrosive stress ends. This is done by flattening the organisational structure and implementing a leaner, more active and hands-on management process.

Flat organisational structures, apart from being a cost reduction, have the benefits of fewer obstructions to the communication flow, reducing the filtering effect of information that a hierarchical structure has, and opening communication lines. Strategy will be discussed and refined not only in more frequent scheduled meetings but in impromptu encounters.

You often see this flattening of structure with a reduction of non-operational or head office roles.

Gaining control

The turnaround leader needs to take control of the turnaround process as quickly as possible. They cannot be effective if instructions are being ignored or are ineffective. There are two strategies to avoid this: widening the span of management control by the turnaround manager and sidelining some of the senior executives. This is discussed below in the personnel section.

Structural change to gain management control is more common with larger businesses. There are three common types of organisational change in turnarounds:

· **Decentralised change**, where the decision-making moves to the operational or business unit managers. Decentralisation is breaking the business into smaller units with managers directly having accountability for those units. It is advantageous in a turnaround to define responsibilities and accountabilities to provide some clarity to confusion or kawdigoo.[32]

- **Centralised change** is the inverse of decentralised and can be an effective structure when the distressed business was decentralised, with the various business units run as mini-fiefdoms. Centralisation in this situation helps bring information back to the turnaround leader rather than being lost or retained in the bowels of a business unit. The treasury or cash management is one area that is often centralised in a turnaround.

- **Umbrella change**, where a group is placed above or over the existing structure. I worked on a turnaround of a publicly listed multinational that had a presence in four countries, and distribution and manufacturing divisions. I was one of six executives 'parachuted' in to manage the turnaround and sit above the existing management team – just long enough to assess the situation and put the right people in place. This is often used by private equity buyouts.

Personnel change

If the turnaround and then the business in the medium to longer term are going to be successful, there need to be appropriate leaders managing the various teams. It needs to be determined if the current staff, and particularly team leaders, have the capability and attitude required during the Crisis Stabilisation phase of the turnaround.

In my book *Run Your Business Better*, a theme was just because you have specific or technical skills – you might be a great electrician, web designer or hairdresser – does not mean you have the business

---

32 An Inuit word meaning *the water has settled clear* – when life gets tangled you follow the river until the chaos falls away.

skills and/or the soft skills required to run a business well or even competently. To successfully manage a business you require technical, business and behaviour capabilities.

All leaders and ideally all staff would self-assess to determine if they have what is required. But seldom is that the case, and the turnaround manager is often required to facilitate the assessment. There are two broad approaches for this assessment.

- **On the bus or off the bus approach.** With this approach the turnaround manager and the business's most senior people (management or board) have a meeting with the staff. They outline in broad terms their turnaround plan and what is required from the staff. The floor is opened for questions and a general discussion about the way forward – and this is where it gets really interesting. The turnaround manager while answering questions is also assessing who is buying into the plan and prepared to work to make it succeed. These are two different factors to consider, as some staff might be prepared to work on the plan but may not be buying into it, and others may be buying into the plan but do not have the energy and willingness to work on it. After the meeting those staff that demonstrated they either did not buy into the turnaround plan or were not prepared to work on the plan will be terminated. I admit this is a fast, brutal, blunt instrument, however people who cannot commit to the turnaround plan will sap time, money and resources away from the activities that need to be completed in this phase of the turnaround process. They will erode the morale of other staff. This assessment is not about their functional capability and does not consider how good they are at the role. It is about how they go about performing their role in a turnaround context.

- **Management critical evaluation approach.** The turnaround manager with the most senior management reviews each staff member from the Chief Executive Officer down. Some questions they may consider in their assessment are:

- Does the staff member understand the difficulties that lie ahead?
- Is there 'congruency of purpose' with the turnaround plan?
- Are they prepared to prioritise resources to deliver the turnaround?
- Are they battle hardened and have weathered other difficult situations?
- Are there gaps in the overall team skillset?
- Can they balance short-term imperatives with medium-term aspirations?
- Are there clicks or factions, or does the entire team work together for mutual support and purpose?
- Is the information flow appropriate for the turnaround?

This approach is not as blunt as the 'on the bus or off the bus' approach, but it is still about determining who is part of the problem or who is going to be a problem in this phase of the turnaround.

With the SpiceJet turnaround, Kapoor assembled the 13 business unit heads and asked them to present on how their business unit was performing. All told Kapoor how well their business unit was doing, showing charts and slides that everything was on the right track. Kapoor then asked them, 'If everyone is rowing in the same forward direction, why is the boat going backwards?' The staff were either in denial or wanted to portray they were competent and deserved to remain in their position. Kapoor then 'shook the tree'. He said to the 13 business unit heads that not all would have positions with SpiceJet. Some of these people may not be the 'right fit' to turn the business around. There was also a great sense that it was not possible to turn the airline around. Kapoor would not accept that it was not possible, when other airlines and other businesses had been turned around. Kapoor believed everything was possible – he just needed to know how long it would take, and how much it would cost. Those who did not believe it was possible exited the business.

Almost all, if not all turnarounds make some change in personnel at this phase of the process. Some of the reasons personnel change is necessary are:

- new skills are necessary
- it helps overcome legacy issues
- poor-performing and weak management needs to be replaced
- it helps restore credibility with all stakeholders – both internal and external
- new management and leaders bring a different energy or vibe that can help bring momentum for the turnaround
- it is a clear signal to all stakeholders that change is happening, and the turnaround is going to be successful!

Employment rewards and conditions

Ansett Australia was a major Australian airline that was put into voluntary administration in 2001, and eventually liquidation in March 2002. Ansett was bleeding cash to the tune of $1.3 million a day. There were many reasons for the demise of Ansett Australia, with the main reasons cited being its parent company, Air New Zealand, paying too much for Ansett in February 2000, the aging fleet, the vast array of aircraft types, and the emergence of low-cost competitor airlines. The structure and remuneration and conditions of the staff – being top heavy and overpaid – was also a substantial reason.

With this structure and remuneration, Ansett faced many hurdles. Ansett floated moving to being a low-cost airline, and also merging with Air New Zealand. It is purported these were thwarted by the strong aviation union wanting to protect the conditions and remuneration of the Australian staff, which was much higher and more generous than other airlines.

Virgin Blue employed 3,300 staff for its domestic operations, compared with Ansett's 10,000.[33] Virgin Blue staff were paid 50% less than Ansett staff. There were instances of three-person cockpit crew levels when the engineer role was superfluous, and guaranteed overtime of 10 hours per week. Baggage handlers were being paid more than level A university lecturers. The report 'The Post-Retrenchment Labour Market Experiences of Ansett Workers' by Webber & Weller (2002) said: 'For better or worse, it is reasonable to conclude that Ansett workers' perceptions of the benefits that employers provide their workforce were becoming increasingly out of step with the conditions of employment in the "flexible" workplaces of discount airlines and in many firms in other industries.' Tom Ballantyne, an aviation commentator in a speech post Ansett's collapse, said, 'The union movement should hang its head in shame at the years of short-sighted money-grabbing that played as big a role in Ansett's death as did the repeated negligence of various owners to the management needs of the airline. It's ironic that both owners and unions essentially saw Ansett as a cash cow and that owners, just as criminally, mostly gave in to union demands.'

In a turnaround it is usual, and often necessary, that remuneration is changed to reflect the condition of the business at that time, and/or to link remuneration with performance. For instance, all staff may be asked to take a pay cut or offered voluntary redundancy.

---

33 Around 16,000 staff if regional and international staff are included.

In an industry like retail, staff remuneration may be in part linked to sales key performance indicators (KPIs), and in manufacturing remuneration may be linked to productivity targets.

Contracts of employment are often renegotiated in a turnaround. KPIs are established to reflect the needs of the turnaround and contracts negotiated to reflect that and remunerate people for achieving the goals required, and not necessarily the historical KPIs.

In larger businesses that are unionised, the behaviour and cooperation of the union can be a defining point in the ability to turn a business around. With Ansett, the strength of the union in obtaining remuneration and rewards for members built a culture where employees believed they had jobs for life, and they were 'fairly' remunerated – even though they were massively out of step with like airlines. Ballantyne said regarding Ansett, 'unions must bear a substantial amount of the blame for Ansett's troubles'.

Chapter 10

Process improvements

In the Analysis phase predictors, signs, symptoms and causes of business distress and decline were discussed. In almost all turnarounds there is a failure of processes, and therefore a requirement to address process deficiencies and improve processes. After all, making no changes will result in no change.

Process change can be either doing things better or doing better things with the resources. The changes are seldom quick fixes, and are therefore part of the Crisis Stabilisation phase of the turnaround process.

Before I discuss specifics, it must first be understood what turnaround process improvement is and is not.

Business turnaround process improvement is different to normal business process re-engineering (BPR). While both result in a business transformation, BPR is a strategy based on aspiration – not only to survive but to thrive. It is a strategy used as part of growing or developing a business – usually a healthy business or as part of a merger/acquisition. Turnaround process improvement, however, is a strategy of need – the need to survive. It is a reactive strategy that allows a business to shift from desperation to aspiration.

With turnaround process improvement options are often limited. As a result process improvement focuses on a few critical systems where change can be enacted quickly, and where there is the biggest 'bang for the buck' – the big impacts of cost cutting, quality improvement and improved customer responsiveness – the three dimensions of turnaround process improvement.

Three dimensions of turnaround process improvement

Cost improvement

All businesses, including distressed businesses short of cash, have processes or activities that are non-value added. This was discussed in the 'Cash' and 'Financial control' sections in the Emergency phase of this book. In the Crisis Stabilisation phase this continues, and expands to look for opportunities to simplify business processes. This might be achieved by process mapping the business and looking at workflows.

Quality improvement

Quality improvement is a structured approach to analysing the performance of systems and processes, and then enacting measures to correct or improve them. There are three characteristics of quality improvements processes:

- Quality improvement focus is on processes, not people.
- Quality improvement is data driven.

- Quality improvement involves people as part of the solution, and looks to identify the people who are directly involved in and best understand the processes of the business.

Quality, or lack thereof, is often a cause of business decline. A product or service that has quality issues usually has declining sales, increased costs, unhappy customers or clients and reputational and opportunity costs.

Time improvement

You have probably heard the saying 'time is money', and this is definitely the case in a distressed business. Time improvement is about making each minute effective. Are there ways to reduce steps in a process? This will reduce some indirect costs, such as managing the process, reducing inventory levels, or reducing funding costs. Time improvements may also increase customer satisfaction.

Chapter 11

Sales and marketing improvements

Most small businesses are not sufficiently big enough to have dedicated sales and marketing teams, so much of this section is for medium to large businesses. However, even in small businesses the lessons and concepts discussed can be applied to some extent; for example, while a small business may not have a dedicated sales and marketing team, there may be one person responsible for sales and a different person, or an outsourced team, responsible for marketing.

There are some universal characteristics of a distressed business's sales and marketing functions. These include:

- inconsistent pricing
- a focus on the number of sales, or sales volume, and not profitability (as discussed earlier)
- lack of knowledge or understanding of competitors
- tensions, misunderstanding of roles and responsibilities, and blame culture between sales and marketing areas

- lack of performance measures
- large, fragmented product line
- aging product line and hardcore
- poorly trained and poorly managed sales team without realistic sales targets or performance measures
- lack of customer care, slow responses to enquiries, and no emphasis on customer experience or delighting customers.

Resolving all these issues will take time and resources – but even in the Crisis Stabilisation phase these are not abundant. Some actions to rectify the above will roll into the Growth phase.

There are five sales and marketing areas of improvement that are addressed in the Crisis Stabilisation phase:

- customer expectations
- pricing
- sales process improvement
- product line rationalisation
- marketing improvements.

Customer expectations

When things start going wrong in a business a 'lord of the flies' situation often ensues. Instead of remembering that the business exists to deliver a product or service to customers or clients, the focus turns inward and finger pointing starts.

The turnaround leader must address this immediately and get information about the customers and clients – their needs, their expectations, their buying behaviour, and their perception of your business compared to your competitors. If this cannot be achieved objectively internally, then an independent external source should be engaged. Staff are often a wealth of information that just needs to be mined – they might also be the customer.

When I am engaged in a turnaround I like to be 'shoulder deep' – and this will mean getting to know the customers, especially the key customers, and for them to meet me too. Often they will tell me things they have been too 'polite' to tell my client. Also, with me meeting them a perception develops that things are going to get better, and there is also some leeway established to 'buy time' to make some changes.

Adjusting pricing

Pricing is a common area that can be easily addressed in many turnarounds. Often the rationale for how the selling price is determined is flawed or nonexistent.

Pricing requires thought and an understanding of your customers or clients, the market, the environment and your competitors. Set your prices too low and you are leaving money on the table. Set your prices too high and nobody will buy your product or service. The right price is the maximum the customer or client is willing to pay. So, what is that right price and how is it determined? You first need to understand the psychology of pricing.

Before setting a price for a product or service, you need to understand what the price indicates to your target customer or client.

Price can indicate quality or value and, subject to having no other information, we look to value first to shed light on the quality. Therefore, products and services that are more expensive are perceived to be better quality, and products and services priced lower are perceived to be of lower quality.

Businesses use price to communicate something about their product or service. They may lower the price to communicate value for money, or raise the price to communicate quality or prestige. Of course, neither of these may be true, but it is a message that the business is trying to communicate.

Pricing also needs to be consistent with the other brand elements. For example, if you are trying to price for exclusivity then the marketing, packaging, sales pitch and so on also need to reflect the exclusivity of the brand.

My rules of pricing psychology are:

- **Pricing should be about value – real or perceived.** Get customers or clients to focus on value and what you can do for them, and they will stop focusing on cost.

- **Focus on how people feel and not how people think.** Connecting with customers or clients will bypass objections and resistance and let you focus on the relationship. It stops you having to justify your price and what you are worth and allows you to sell to people.

- **How you communicate with customers and clients affects the pricing.** The setting, atmosphere and your ability to pay attention to the details communicates to the customer or clients and sets their expectations.

- **Customers and clients are not rational.** Keep in mind pricing needs to reflect people's behaviours.

With pricing psychology in mind, in a turnaround there are two quick actions to consider with regards to price – increasing prices and reducing discounts.

Increasing prices

When I started the turnaround process at Andy's mechanical engineering business, one of the first things I did was raise the labour rates, and then again three months later, and nine months after that, and five months after that. Why? What the workshop was doing was specialised and bespoke, but the rates reflected a backyard mechanic. The business also had nil gross margin. Interestingly, two years later the conversations about pricing are such that it's about the type of customers and projects the business wants to attract, and what they want to be known for as a business, rather than worrying (irrationally, in my opinion) that customers will go elsewhere. But this irrational fear is not uncommon. So, to determine how much and on what products to increase prices, there needs to be some analysis of competition and customers. Let's look at Andy's business and how I did a rough analysis:

- While there were several competitors in the vehicle restoration industry where Andy was, his business's competitive advantage was they did all areas of the restoration – mechanical, design, engineering, fabrication and metal shaping. Others only did some of those functions.

- Vehicle restoration is a long process and may take a couple of years to complete. Also, the vehicles are a function of the time they were built so the materials may be non-compliant nowadays. And, as the project unfolds, new issues arise such as rust in an area that cannot be seen at first glance. Therefore, to undertake these projects the customer needs deep pockets (and patience).

- Wait time to get a vehicle into the workshop was long, so once a vehicle was in the workshop the customer was unlikely to take it out as it might be years before they can get back in.

- Most workshops that do maintenance-type jobs – in and out in a day – charged 2.5 times an hour what Andy was charging. This in part reflects their ad hoc nature and the possibility that not every hour of staff time was able to be charged out. So, this was the ceiling for price, and Andy should be charging somewhere in between.

• Andy's customers knew all the above – they would have done their homework.

This analysis showed that prices could be increased, and absolutely *should* be increased.

Andy had made some common pricing mistakes. Pricing mistakes can be put down to two broad issues: mistakes with pricing psychology, and pricing strategy mistakes.

Pricing psychology mistake

There is a concept known as the pricing paradox (sometimes called the water–diamond paradox). With the water–diamond paradox, we understand that water is necessary to our life and that ornaments such as diamonds are not life-sustaining. But water typically has a low market price, while diamond jewellery has a high market price. The reason is due to what is known as 'marginal utility'; price is based on the value or utility someone places on a product. Consumers will pay based on their perceived value or utility, at a point and place in time. Consumers do not consider your business's circumstances, business environment or competition when deciding if they will pay the price for your product or service.

Common pricing strategy mistakes

Unfortunately, pricing is a bit like magic – there is no formula that works for you, me and a particular group. Price needs to consider situations, costs, competition, strategy and environment. However, there are a few common pricing strategy mistakes, and forewarned is forearmed:

- **Pricing based on cost rather than value.** How much did you pay for your morning coffee today? $4 for a long black? If the barista were to base the price on cost, you may have paid only $1!

- **Set-and-forget pricing.** When was the last time you updated your pricing? The customers are 'happy' with the current pricing (of course they are!) and 'if it ain't broke, don't fix it' ... right?

- **Same margin for all products or services.** Using the coffee example above, if I were to apply the same margin to the muffin I bought with the coffee, the muffin would cost about $18.

- **Discounting.** Discounting (discussed more below) without understanding the ramifications is a dangerous game. A 10% discount to the sales price can lead to a lot larger impact on the bottom line. Discounting also communicates something to the customer and also sets their expectations.

- **Price following.** Businesses that price follow often do not understand their customers, or their market segmentation, or their product or service value.

- **Blaming lack of sales on price.** Nine times out of ten a lack of sales has more to do with a marketing and sales problem than a price problem. In a customer buyer journey, price is a long way along the journey. Awareness, informing and educating – all part of the marketing that occurs well before the sale is made or the price is discussed. Have you tried buying a car recently? You are well down the track before the salesperson will crunch the numbers and tell you the price.

- **Thinking customers cannot afford to pay full price.** If I am working on a recovery engagement and were to think that XYZ Pty Ltd are in dire straits and could not afford me then I would end up working for free. If your product is well out of your customers' market (you're trying to sell BMWs to pensioners)

then you are confusing your value proposition or your
target market.

- **Pricing too low.** This is different to low pricing – but you need
to know how low is too low. The only customers that love too
low prices are the crap customers – the ones you do not want.
The ones you want just get confused and/or suspicious – these
customers understand value and want to feel unique. Price
needs to make sense to your target market.

- **Options – too many or too few.** Some businesses make the
mistake of providing too many pricing tiers, while others
make the mistake of providing too few. The correct amount of
pricing tiers for your business will align with your unique buyer
personas. Options mistakes extend to payment options too.
The recent trend is services such as 'Afterpay' and 'Zippay' and
credit and pay services such as 'Square Up'.

- **Price to optimise profit.** A buyer of your product or service
pays the price they value your product or service at. The buyer
does not consider your costs. The price should, however, always
be greater than the minimum cost to provide your product
or service.

- **Does your price match your brand?** Consider your brand and
what that brand is trying to portray to the market. If your product
or service is a discount or low value brand, then the price should
reflect that. Conversely, if your product or service is prestigious
or exclusive then the price should also reflect that.

Reducing discounts

The second quick action to consider with regards to price is to change
discounts. Discounts are customer-centric – and therefore should
be used to drive a particular customer behaviour. Cutting discounts

should be carefully considered before implementation in a turn-around situation. There are two common types of discounts – volume discounts and price discounts. Volume discounts are more common in a distribution business, price discounts in a retail business.

Increasing or decreasing discounts can increase or decrease volume in sales, so you need to do an analysis as to the overall change to the business by changing the discounts. For example, increasing a discount may increase sales volume or reduce the days to receive the cash. This might be detrimental to the cashflow but improve the profit margin. Consider if cashflow is more important than profit at this time.

Discounts can also be used to direct customer behaviour and to change the customer mix. Using consulting firms as an example, the hourly rate charged is often high, however clients that sign up for a longer period or on a retainer basis are charged a fixed or retainer rate which usually equates to a lower rate than the hourly rate. The consulting firm is wanting long-term, regular fee clients rather than short-term ad hoc clients that require higher compliance and marketing costs and value the result over the relationship.

Discounts can also be used in a turnaround situation to exit unprofitable product or service lines, or clear slow-moving inventory to generate cash that can be better employed in the business – such as paying down debt or investing in other products or services.

Usually, the greatest objection to reducing discounts (or increasing prices) comes from the sales department. They have a belief that it will make it harder to make sales, and often their remuneration is also tied to sales. Therefore, it is important to listen to the sales department before changing discounts, and then communicate why either raising prices or changing discounts is required and what is expected from those changes.

Improving the sales process

Though it may appear counterintuitive, increasing the volume of sales can be the wrong strategy in the Crisis Stabilisation phase of a turnaround. This is because increasing sales volume requires investment of time, money, people and processes. Time and money are scarce resources at this stage, so the focus should be on the sales process, ensuring efforts are towards the right and profitable product lines, and the right people are in place to execute the sales strategy.

After the Chief Financial Officer, the Head of Sales is probably the most important role in most turnarounds, and it is imperative that the right person is in this position. However, it does not always follow a good salesperson makes a good sales manager.

Product line rationalisation

A proliferation of products is often a characteristic of underperforming businesses, so in a turnaround this requires some rationalisation. Underperforming product lines need to be discontinued. A generic guide for this is:

- Bespoke, custom made or frequently modified for the customer products are rarely profitable and are time consuming at every stage of the process from selling, production, delivery to after-sales care.

- Products with declining sales and/or declining profitability should be discontinued or the selling price should be raised.

- If a product has a negative gross margin, discontinue selling it.

- Products below a set gross margin should also be discontinued; for example, if a product's gross margin was 5% but the overheads were 10% you may consider discontinuing this product.

- Products that are capital intensive and low margin should be discontinued.

Rationalisation of products can be met with resistance, but it can also free up cash tied up in inventories, reduce operating costs, release capital through the sale of machinery and focus the sales team on the profitable products only. Remember, we are mending a distressed business – when the company is healthy again, products can be reviewed for their strategic importance.

Marketing improvements

The last part of the sales process improvement is to look at the marketing investment and its effectiveness. In a healthy business, marketing is a good and necessary investment, however in a healthy business there is also the luxury of time. Marketing seldom has instantaneous results, and in a turnaround situation where time and cash are scarce marketing costs can be implemented quickly without an immediate impact on sales. Furthermore, through product rationalisation the marketing focus and perhaps the quantum also changes, so the whole marketing strategy and direction requires analysis and a rethink.

It is also a fallacy that if you do not market the business then you will have no sales or less sales. One business I was engaged to turn around had a pipeline that went out many years without spending a cent on marketing. However, the decision was made that towards the end of the Crisis Stabilisation phase there would be some marketing with the desired outcome to change the type of customer rather than increase sales.

Chapter 12
Operational efficiency improvements

In most, if not all businesses and particularly in distressed businesses there are operational inefficiencies. This applies to all types of businesses from sole trader Larry the Landscaper to multinational manufacturing businesses.[34]

The broad term I use for operational inefficiencies is 'leakage', as it represents things that result in less-than-optimal cashflow or profitability. These may be time, effort, cash or material, or a combination of these.

Improving operational efficiency as part of a business turnaround process is to streamline and systemise processes and eliminate redundant processes and waste. Operational efficiency improvement is important because:

---

34 Operational efficiency is usually a discussion in the context of a manufacturing business. A whole book could be written on operational efficiency in manufacturing, but the focus of this book is on turnarounds – of all types, sizes and industries. As such, this book will have a more generic discussion on operational efficiency.

- **It optimises cash and time.** In a turnaround, both cash and time are scarce so there is a need to optimise these two resources. I have explained earlier my decision criteria of 'like, want or need'. With cash and time, start with this question – is it a like, a want or a need?
- **It can boost profitability.** Eliminating redundant processes, tightening operational processes, managing time and systemising processes will boost profitability.
- **It can increase the value of the business.** A business that uses its resources efficiently is more profitable and therefore more valuable, but in addition, if there is automation or systemisation the business is not reliant on particular individuals and becomes more valuable again.
- **It helps determine future opportunities.** In reviewing and refining the operational processes, new ways of doing things may be identified, competitive advantages uncovered, and new products or services recognised.
- **It will help the business last longer.** A business that is operationally efficient is profitable longer and also has a greater capacity to weather downturns, competitor gains and financial hurdles.
- **It increases growth potential.** Optimising the operational process adds capacity and increases productivity. These gains can be utilised to grow the business, and the productivity gains can be used to reward the current staff and attract new staff.

How to improve operational efficiency

Here are six steps to improve operational efficiency:

1. **Stop the leaks.** Review the processes and conduct some financial analysis. This may take many forms depending on the type of

business. With Andy's mechanical engineering business, we have discussed the Friday lunches and not charging for consumables. Other leaks were several unused software subscriptions and other such overhead costs, and processes on the workshop floor. There was a time leak too. There was no onboarding process, so time was being spent on this during projects.

2. **Focus on core processes.** Nine out of ten times the core processes are the ones that make the most for your business and carry the reputation of the business. Understand what is core, and make sure everyone gets that right all the time. This might be something as seemingly insignificant as how the phone is answered, or how the solution for a coating is mixed. People gravitate to new and exciting – be conscious of this and direct them back to nailing the core before jumping to the new or non-core processes.

3. **Technology is not always a silver bullet.** My father worked in a department store, but it was very 'old-fashioned' as it did not have cash registers (this was pre-computers and internet). They had a 'Lamson' system – a series of vacuum tubes that sent cash to a central spot and the cashier would send back the change.[35] When I queried why they had not moved to a cash register on every counter the store owners gave me the following explanation:

- If the process works then consider carefully why it should change.
- The time it took to send the monies to the cash desk and the change to return was used to wrap the parcel (yes, in paper

---

35 Lamson pneumatic tube systems are still used today to transport items, including in the healthcare industry (lab results, samples, etc.), casinos, supermarkets, and some industrial and distribution businesses that cover large areas.

and string in those days). It would take longer with a cash register to both manage the register and wrap the parcel.

- There were better controls on the cash, and the cash was more secure and staff were safer as there was no cash at the counter.

A client's new manager tried to implement an electronic task and time system.[36] This sounded great, but they failed to understand the existing process and the skills and abilities of the production staff with technology. The trial failed miserably. Updating technology needs to be carefully considered and the implementation needs to be managed properly.

4. **Understand the corporate culture.** When trying to implement a process change, understand there may be a generational divide that needs to be bridged. The management team may be from one generation (for example, Gen X) and the 'worker bees' from a different generation (for example, millennials). One of the most forgotten differences is the preference of communication of different generations. As mentioned earlier, my kids do not read emails or make phone calls – they prefer messages and chats, whereas I prefer emails and phone calls.

5. **Flatten the structure.** As discussed previously, a decentralised structure can lead to a more collaborative process. This collaboration can add speed and agility to the process, whereas a vertical structure of command and control is more bureaucratic. When a question arises in a flat structure everybody hears it at the same time, and the response is team based as opposed to function based.

---

36 The trial also occurred in the Emergency phase of the turnaround and therefore the timing was inappropriate.

6. **Systemise the business.** Josh Kaufman in his book *The Personal MBA: Master the art of business* describes systems as: '... a process made explicit and repeatable – a series of steps that has been formalised in some way. Systems can be written or diagrammed, but they are always externalised in some way. The primary benefit of creating a system is that you can examine the process and make improvements. By making each step in the process explicit, you can understand how the core processes work, how they are structured, how they affect other processes and systems, and how you can improve the system over time.' In fact, most internationally well-known business gurus and authors espouse the same message, though usually from the perspective of developing a business rather than a turnaround.

Information and performance management

It is almost a certainty that a distressed business does not have good, reliable, accurate and timely information or a performance management structure. This includes financial information, production information, KPIs for staff, employment records and corporate records; for example, ASIC and ATO records, inventory and costs systems, or marketing and sales information. In doing so they are running 'blind', with nothing to base decisions on or evaluate progress from decisions that are made.

Reliable information is required to make informed decisions and manage performance. Staff behaviours and performance cannot be objectively assessed, changed or rewarded without having good information, so processes to obtain this information need to be put in place as part of the business process improvement. It is after all the people who are going to execute the turnaround strategy.

Chapter 13

Financial restructuring

Financial restructuring is a range of processes to change the financial structure of the business. It focuses on the capital structure of the business (both debt and equity), the cash-generation and debt-carrying ability, and the valuation of the business and its components. It is a vital step in stabilising the distressed business.

Financial restructuring starts with a review of the capital structure and the balance sheet. It then assesses both the appropriateness of the type of financing and the magnitude of the financing. It will also look at the economic value of parts of the business and the use of capital within them. It may entail a wide range of actions, such as renegotiating debts, selling assets and changing the business's capital (debt and equity) structure. The goal of financial restructuring is to improve the business's liquidity, reduce its debt burden and improve its cashflow. Financial restructuring also assists in regaining trust of stakeholders, particularly creditors and investors. It also provides a platform for the company to build on.

There are usually two stages of financial restructuring: short-term financial restructuring where the focus is on just surviving or 'buying time', and longer term financial restructuring where the aim is to make a platform for the business to stabilise, then grow.

The objectives of financial restructuring are:

- Restoring solvency using both the cashflow and balance sheet tests of solvency.

- Having a capital structure (debt and equity) that is appropriate to the forecast levels of cashflow.

- Ensuring enough funds are available – both existing and new sources – to finance the turnaround.

Short-term financial restructuring

Short-term financial restructuring occurs in the Emergency phase and was discussed earlier.

There are three steps involved in short-term financial restructuring: establishing the current financial position, establishing what the future looks like for the business, and then developing a case for support.

Establishing the current financial position

Establishing the current financial position starts with analysing the current liabilities to creditors and funders and the terms of those arrangements. Usually this is not in one place or in a format easily understandable. Put a table together as shown below.

Supplier/ funder	Current amount owing	Total credit facility	Security	Term	Contact person

Then sort the table by those that have security and those that do not.

Determining the short to medium future funding requirements

With a cashflow forecast and a turnaround and strategic plan at hand, endorsed by the owners or board, the funding gap or requirements can be established, and importantly validated. At this stage the owners or board need to be mindful of solvency – it may be appropriate to look at Safe Harbour provisions (see below). I would recommend that decisions and considerations of boards at this stage are well documented, and the plan is regularly reviewed until a financial restructuring agreement is in place.

Developing a case for support

Financial restructuring assists in regaining trust of stakeholders, particularly creditors and investors. Creditors and investors are much more likely to support your business if you come armed with a well-thought-out case for support, and if you conduct discussions with openness, transparency and goodwill. It is also preferable to meet them in person, as this helps build or establish a relationship. Body language is also important at these meetings, so be mindful of how you dress, your manners, tone of voice and how you sit or stand.

Longer term financial restructuring

The objectives of longer term financial restructuring are to provide a platform to stabilise and grow the business and restore creditor and funder confidence. This is achieved with a solvent balance sheet and executing an agreed turnaround plan and strategy.

Creditors and funders will need to be satisfied that:

- The business will be stabilised and viable.

- There is an expectation that value will be restored for existing shareholders while providing an adequate return to debt holders.
- The funders or creditors will get their monies back.
- The right management team are in place who can execute the turnaround.
- The plan provides a reasonable expectation of a better outcome for the business than immediate administration or liquidation.

There should be an atmosphere of congeniality among stakeholders where all are willing to work together to make the business stable and viable. Equity holders also need to expect that their ownership will be diluted, and the return on their investment is reliant on the support of the debtholders, and that return may be lower than they would like or expect for a protracted period.

There are two typical longer term financial restructuring strategies. There is capital restructuring, which is changing the mix of and levels of debt and equity of the business. This may be through converting some or all of the bank's or financier's debt to equity,[37] capitalising unpaid interest into the loan (or equity), consolidating debt facilities to extend the repayment period and/or lower the average interest costs, issuing new equity such as rights issues, options, private placements or preference shares, or new debt/borrowings. Renegotiation of debt takes time and energy, and can redirect attention and focus away from the overall turnaround strategy. As it also directly impacts shareholders, it is often useful to have a board member run point on the negotiations and liaise between the funders, the shareholders and the turnaround leader.

The second typical longer term financial restructuring strategy is an asset reduction strategy. This can quickly reduce debt and

---

37 Often, and in particular in family businesses, there is a related party loan that may need to be converted into equity, as in substance it is equity rather than a loan.

provide cash. Look for assets that are surplus to requirements or add no or minimum value to the business. Also look at assets for which the repairs, maintenance and 'holding' costs are greater than replacing with a newer, better model. For example, the business may have an old van with a book value of $6,000 and you foresee the repairs and maintenance costs over the next few years (including downtime while getting repaired) are $10,000. You may consider buying a newer van for, say, $18,000, which you borrow the monies for, and sell the old van for $9,000. Your immediate cashflow is improved by $9,000 and the loan repayments are less than the forecast repairs and maintenance costs. The $9,000 can be used to either pay down debt – be it for the new van, or other debt that is strategically more critical – or to provide immediate working capital.

Part IV

FORMAL INSOLVENCY OPTIONS

This book is about turning around and saving businesses, however for context and awareness, this section gives an overview of formal insolvency options available in Australia and New Zealand.[38] Unfortunately not every business can be saved.

In both Australia and New Zealand formal insolvency is creditor-centric – it is for the benefit of creditors and the process is funded by the creditors. Overseas, the insolvency process is predominately debtor-centric – for the benefit of the business to keep operating, with a broad church of beneficiaries.

The current formal insolvency processes in Australia and New Zealand seldom result in businesses surviving or provide a reset for the businesses. The vast majority of businesses that enter formal insolvency end up being liquidated and cease to exist. There are no 'winners' – creditors will end up with less, shareholders will end up with nothing, employees will lose their jobs and often unpaid entitlements, and directors may be personally liable for some of the debts of the business. Even the insolvency practitioner seldom gets paid for the entire amount of time and costs incurred on the engagement.

There are also professional conflict of interest issues with the customer-centric models. Business owners should be aware of this when presented with formal insolvency options. Some of the pre-insolvency options and actions available are not pursued by

---

38 This information is correct at the time of writing (May 2023). Legislation changes, so if you do need to go down this route, make sure you get up-to-date information.

insolvency practitioners as this would scope them out of potential formal insolvency actions later. There is also a conflict of interest that is allowed in that the formal insolvency practitioner is being paid by the creditors and will only take action and various options if funds are forthcoming from the creditors. While this is not hidden and is declared, it is still a conflict of interest – real, potential and perceived.

Chapter 14

When is a business insolvent?

Formal insolvency actions can start when a business is insolvent, but at what point is a business insolvent?

> ❛ Insolvency as defined by ASIC as 'when a company or person can't pay debts when they are due'.

Insolvency as defined by ASIC as 'when a company or person can't pay debts when they are due'. There are two usual tests used to confirm if a business is insolvent – the cashflow test that looks at whether your business can pay its liabilities, as and when they fall due, and the balance sheet test that works out whether your business would have more assets or liabilities if it were immediately wound up. It is important to do both tests as the cashflow test focuses on timing and the balance sheet test focuses on quantum. For example, by looking at the balance sheet test a business may have more liabilities than assets, but dovetailing in the cashflow test will show that the loans are to a related party that is unlikely to call in the loan on the due date, therefore the business is not actually insolvent. Conversely the balance sheet test may show more assets than liabilities, however the cashflow test shows that the debts cannot be paid when they fall due; for instance, the business may own property but be unable to liquidate it quickly enough to pay debts when they fall due.

Chapter 15

Pre-insolvency and options

Safe Harbour

Safe Harbour is a defence under the Corporations Act in Australia that allows some relief against a director's duty to prevent a company trading while insolvent. New Zealand does not have a Safe Harbour provision in its Companies Act. Safe Harbour is only available to incorporated companies (so not sole traders, trading trusts or partnerships).

Under this provision, with the supervision of an 'appropriately qualified advisor', the directors formulate a plan to turn the company around that will be reasonably likely to lead to a better outcome for the company than immediate administration or liquidation. Directors remain in control of the company. This process is conducted behind the scenes.

Safe Harbour promotes directors taking reasonable steps to trade the company out of financial difficulty without concerns about personal liability, or affecting the potential value of the company by prematurely appointing a voluntary administrator. Safe Harbour promotes a cultural change within the boardroom to try to turn the company around.

The Australian Government when enacting the legislation said it was aimed at fostering a business culture of entrepreneurship and moving away from an environment that penalises business failure. Essentially the Safe Harbour provisions allow the directors to be 'safe harboured' from the personal liability insolvency provisions in the Corporations Act. They will not be personally liable for loss or damage a creditor suffers in relation to a debt, provided certain conditions are met.

A pre-pack arrangement

A pre-pack arrangement is a legally binding agreement to rescue an insolvent business. It is a sale process where the business assets, or the whole business, are sold prior to the appointment of an insolvency practitioner. The insolvency practitioner would review the sale terms and if appropriate ratify the sale agreement.

Pre-pack agreements 'phoenix' distressed businesses, and while in countries like the United Kingdom pre-pack agreements are both common and legitimate, in Australia and New Zealand they are frowned upon. There is little understanding of how to perform a pre-pack, and a lot of discussion in the media and government agencies regarding illegal phoenixing.

So, let me explain what a phoenix company is. A phoenix company is a company that 'rises from the ashes' of a failed or insolvent company. It is established to carry on the business of the failed or insolvent company using the assets and employing the staff, but not taking on the failed or insolvent business's liabilities. Usually, the shareholders and directors are the same as the failed or insolvent company. The new company rises from the burden of liabilities of the old company and the creditors are left to recover what they can from the old company. Now this sounds very bad – as the creditors are left with nothing.

Phoenixing can be both legal and illegal – I make the distinction by calling pre-pack arrangements legal phoenixing. The characteristics of *illegal* phoenixing are there is little or no consideration paid by the new company for the old company's assets, and there is no plan to repay all or some of the outstanding liabilities such as creditors, taxes, superannuation or employee entitlements. Illegal phoenixing is also bad and unfair for competitors. The phoenix company is avoiding paying its debts and lowering its cost base, giving it an unfair advantage such that competitors cannot match it with pricing. There are a number of provisions in the Corporations Act that are designed to prevent some of the characteristics of illegal phoenixing such as uncommercial transactions, unreasonable director-related transactions and transactions to defeat creditors. There are also director duty provisions that require directors to act in good faith and for proper purpose. However, illegal phoenixing is rampant, and there are seldom prosecutions against the people involved. This has resulted in *any* phoenix activity being regarded as illegal (even if it is not)!

Pre-pack advisors, however, conduct the phoenix sale agreement in a lawful manner. There are three steps in Australia to conducting a pre-pack arrangement.

1. **Preparation.**
   - Directors should have all assets (and/or the business) valued by an independent, registered valuer. The sale of assets will be based on the fair market price provided by the valuer.
   - No new non-essential debt can be incurred.

2. **Execution.**

- A conditional contract to sell the asset or business at fair market price is executed.
- The conditional contract allows the business to continue to operate under licence.
- The contract is subject to ratification by the insolvency practitioner, who would in due course seek input from the creditors.

3. **Ratification.**

- The directors appoint an Administrator (enter voluntary administration), who as a matter of course would investigate the sale, test the market, and then make a report to the creditors.
- If the creditors support the sale and it is ratified the Administrator will complete the conditional contract. If, however, the sale is not ratified the responsibility for operating and putting another proposal to creditors is that of the Administrator. This may result in a Deed of Company Arrangement or the appointment of a liquidator.

There are some advantages to a pre-pack rather than going straight to voluntary administration:

- It allows experienced turnaround advisors to work with the directors to attempt to save the business.
- It ensures the continuation of the business.
- It can preserve goodwill in the business, and that of its suppliers and customers.
- It can maximise the value of the assets (sum of the parts of distressed assets is less than the sum of the whole). In contrast, illegal phoenixing results in no asset value available to creditors.

- Creditors have the comfort of knowing the sale agreement is still subject to review by the Administrator and requires ratification by the creditors and Administrator.

There are also some risks for the directors and the company:

- The company will still be put in voluntary administration and an Administrator will be appointed. There is a real cost for the Administrator and consequential costs when the Administrator does their investigations and tests the market.

- The directors can still be exposed to potential claims under the Corporations Act; for example, insolvent trading claims.

- The directors may need to consider putting forward a Deed of Company Arrangement as part of the pre-pack.

- The shareholders and directors of the new company will have to arrange funding for the fair market value of the assets or business, and ongoing working capital. Sourcing the funding may not be feasible.

Chapter 16

Insolvency processes and options

Small business restructuring

The Australian Federal Government introduced the Small Business Restructuring Process (SBRP) in January 2021. It allows small businesses in financial distress to access a streamlined, cost-effective process to restructure their debts while the directors remain in control of the business.

To be eligible for the SBRP the following conditions must be met:

- must be a company (not a sole trader, partnership or trading trust)
- total liabilities (excluding employee entitlements) must be under $1 million when entering the Small Business Restructuring Process
- no director, or past director in the prior 12 months, can have been a director of another company that has been under restructuring or simplified liquidation within the preceding seven years

- directors must declare they believe the company has entered into a voidable transaction, and that there are reasonable grounds for believing the company qualifies to propose a Small Business Restructuring Plan
- directors must resolve that the business is insolvent or likely to become insolvent, and a Small Business Restructuring Practitioner be appointed
- appoint a SBRP to oversee the restructuring work, including working with the directors to develop a debt restructuring plan and restructuring proposal statement, all due and payable employee entitlements, including superannuation, must be paid before a restructuring plan can be put to creditors by the directors
- all tax lodgements must be up to date; however, tax debts do not need to all be paid.

The Small Business Restructuring Process is also a quick process, taking 35 days or less. The first step is the proposal or plan is developed to present to the creditors. Directors have 20 days from Small Business Restructuring Process commencement to develop this plan.[39] During this period and while the plan is being developed, trading continues as normal. Creditors are, however, notified the company has entered the process. The SBRP then provides the creditors with the plan and creditors have 15 days to submit a vote to accept or reject the plan.

For the plan to be accepted more than 50% of voting creditors by value (excluding related-party creditors) must vote for the plan. Also, all creditors, regardless of if they voted or how they voted, will be bound by the plan if accepted. When the plan is accepted

---

39 The Small Business Restructuring Practitioner can extend this by a further 10 days under certain circumstances.

the directors remain in place and the restructuring commences and creditors are paid on a pro-rata basis per the timeframes outlined in the plan. Once the payments are made per the plan the company is released from all creditor debts that were subject to the plan.

If the plan is rejected the Small Business Restructuring Process stops, and the directors must consider other options such as voluntary administration or liquidation.

The benefits of the Small Business Restructuring Process are:

- The company retains control over the operations of the business throughout the restructure.
- For creditors there is a likelihood they will recover a portion of monies owed to them.
- For employees all their entitlements that are due must be paid.
- During the process a personal guarantee cannot be enforced against a director or one of their relatives.
- From the commencement of the Small Business Restructuring Process all unsecured and some secured creditors are prohibited from acting against the company to recover money and/or collect property (including terminating contracts and formal debt recovery proceedings).
- It is a quicker, less costly and lower paperwork process than voluntary administration or liquidation.
- Small Business Restructuring plans are being favourably looked on by creditors. They like that there is a real restructure being undertaken with proactive steps to change and improve the business.
- If successful, the business is saved, jobs are saved, suppliers, advisors and service providers retain their customers, and creditors receive a return.

However, there are some risks and downsides to the Small Business Restructuring Process:

- There is an eligibility requirement to have all tax lodgements up to date. Often this is not the case for distressed businesses, and it is both costly and time consuming to get the lodgements up to date.

- Another requirement is to have all employee entitlements paid, including superannuation. Often this is not the case with a distressed business.

- While creditors cannot act on personal guarantees given during the Small Business Restructuring Process, this does not provide for debts that a director has provided a personal guarantee for.

- The rules relating to lockdown director penalty notices will still apply to companies utilising the Small Business Restructuring Process. Directors issued with director penalty notices will continue to be liable even after placing the business in the Small Business Restructuring Process. The ATO can also issue lockdown director penalty notices after the business has been successfully restructured under the Small Business Restructuring Process.

- The Small Business Restructuring Process may cause problems for construction businesses in Queensland that hold a licence issued by the Queensland Building and Construction Commission (QBCC). A company may lose its license because of small business restructuring as the QBCC may assess that it no longer meets the minimum financial requirements for licencing.

- There is a declaration of insolvency, and some creditors and suppliers may decide not to continue supporting the company during the Small Business Restructuring Process.

Simplified Liquidation Process

Like the Small Business Restructuring Process, the Simplified Liquidation Process is an option for small businesses that reduces the cost, time and paperwork required to liquate their company. It is a type of creditors' voluntary liquidation and can be utilised if a company meets the following criteria:

- The company must be unable to pay its debts in full within 12 months after the liquidation commences.
- Total liabilities (excluding contingent liabilities) must be under $1 million.
- All tax lodgements must be up to date.
- No director, or past director in the prior 12 months can have been a director of another company that has been under Simplified Liquidation or Small Business Restructuring Process within the preceding seven years.
- Within five business days of the Simplified Liquidation commencing, the directors must provide a report on the company's affairs and also a declaration that the company meets the Simplified Liquidation eligibility criteria.

A Simplified Liquidation can be commenced by:

- the creditors of the company resolving to voluntarily wind the company up
- the creditors of a company in administration resolving to voluntarily wind the company up
- a company in administration failing to execute a Deed of Company Arrangement (DOCA) in the prescribed timeframe
- the creditors of a company in administration resolving to terminate a DOCA
- the Court orders the termination of a DOCA.

Voluntary Administration

Voluntary Administration is a formal insolvency process where the directors of an insolvent company appoint an Administrator.[40] The Administrator assumes control of the company and the directors' powers are suspended. The purpose of the Voluntary Administration is to provide an alternative to immediately placing the company into liquidation, and for an independent person to protect the going concern value of the company. Over a period of about six weeks the Administrator firstly decides whether the day-to-day trading of the company continues, and while assessing the company and business, they also attempt to develop a plan to put to the creditors that will provide them with greater value than immediate liquidation.

If a plan that provides a better outcome for creditors can be developed the directors will offer this to the creditors. This is known as a Deed of Company Arrangement. If the creditors accept the DOCA the Administrator will oversee the terms in the DOCA and the directors will regain control of the company. If a DOCA cannot be developed or the DOCA is rejected by the creditors the company is placed into liquidation.

However, in Australia Voluntary Administration, especially for smaller companies, has not had a lot of success. Of the companies that enter Voluntary Administration only about a third present a DOCA to the creditors, and less than 5% have their DOCA accepted by the creditors. But that is not the end of the story – of the 5% that have their DOCA accepted, less than 30% end up saving the business, with the remainder just managing to settle the matter outside the liquidation process.

Voluntary Administrations are also expensive, with the fees to the Administrator averaging around $50,000, the return to creditors

---

40 The Voluntary Administration process is largely the same in Australia and New Zealand.

from a successful DOCA averaging around five cents on the dollar of debt owed, and the Administrator's fees increasing further with a successful DOCA.

One of the major failings of the DOCA process though is the Administrator administrates the DOCA and the payments to creditors. They are paid by the creditors and their only responsibility is to secure the best return for the creditors on the debts owing. They do not perform a business turnaround and work shoulder-deep with the business and the directors that make the company sustainable going forward. These are the same directors that oversaw the company into distress.

Liquidation

Liquidation is a process to wind the company up, end its financial affairs and dismantle its corporate structure. An independent person (the Liquidator) is appointed to manage the process and protect the interests of the creditors, directors and shareholders. There are two typical scenarios for a company liquidation. The shareholders may decide the company has come to the end of its useful life, or the company is insolvent and either the directors or creditors decide to wind the company up.[41]

To wind up an insolvent company either the creditors apply to the court to appoint a Liquidator or the directors pass a resolution to appoint a liquidator. For the court to appoint a Liquidator and begin the liquidation process the applicant (a creditor) must demonstrate that the company is insolvent or has undertaken an act that would deem the company insolvent. The directors of an insolvent

---

41 Liquidation is the only way to completely end a company's existence. Deregistered companies can be reinstated via court orders, or by directors and shareholders at time of deregistration.

company can also resolve to place the company in liquidation and appoint a liquidator.

The Liquidator's role is to:

- identify and protect the assets of the company
- sell those assets
- investigate the financial affairs of the company and investigate any suspicious transactions, and if appropriate make any recoveries on such transactions
- prepare reports for regulatory bodies (for example, ASIC)
- distribute funds to the creditors
- return any surplus funds to the shareholders (a rare occurrence with insolvent companies)
- deregister the company.

The Liquidator upon appointment takes control of the company and the directors' authority ceases.

It is important to note that the rights of secured creditors are not affected by the liquidation process, however unsecured creditors' rights to recover monies owed to them cease and they only have a right to a distribution of surplus funds after secured creditors are paid, the Liquidator is paid and employee entitlements are paid.

Receivership

Receivership is a court-mandated tool that creditors holding a registered security interest over an asset can use to recover funds they are owed.[42] Creditors appoint a Receiver (manager) to take control of the asset, sell the asset or protect the rights of the creditor.

A Receiver is typically appointed when the registered assets are under threat because of the risk of insolvency. It may also be

---

42 Typically, it is a bank or other financial institution that appoints a Receiver.

appropriate to appoint a Receiver when the company is going or has gone into Voluntary Administration or Liquidation, or where there is a business subject to the security needing to be operated.

Unlike with Voluntary Administration and Liquidation, the directors remain in control of the business and have the usual director statutory obligations. The Receiver only has authority and management powers insofar as they relate to the security. In practical terms the security is usually over all assets, so the Receiver does assume control and management of the business.

Part XIV Compromises

The New Zealand Companies Act provides an opportunity for insolvent companies to continue and save a business that is a good business but laden with debts. It is an alternative to liquidation, receivership or administration.

Two features are the company will pay back all, or an agreed amount of, the debts over an agreed period, and the remaining debts, if any, are written off. All debts are also frozen and any legal action regarding the debts is suspended during the compromise period.

A Provisional Trustee is appointed and the court notified that a compromise has been proposed. To be accepted, 75% of creditors in number and value must accept the compromise. Once approved by creditors it must also be approved by the court. The Trustee administers the compromise agreement and makes distributions to creditors per the compromise agreement.

Chapter 17

Sole trader or personal insolvency processes and options

In Australia and New Zealand there is different legislation for businesses that are not incorporated as companies. This is hugely problematic for providing the support needed for businesses in distress. It makes it confusing for business owners to understand their options, and to navigate the legislative options is ultimately more expensive.

> ❝ In Australia and New Zealand there is different legislation for businesses that are not incorporated as companies.

There is also a massive chasm in the attention from lawmakers, industry associations and media, with the focus squarely on incorporated company distress and not on the types of businesses that there are far more of, and also that are far more likely to end up in distress.

To illustrate, in Australia only 37.3% of construction businesses are in a company structure. Almost all the remainder are sole trader businesses. Extrapolating the insolvency statistics over the number of constructions companies, just over 1% enter formal insolvency each year, and this percentage is actually decreasing. The number of construction companies is increasing by around 25,000 per annum, while the number of insolvencies is fairly stable at 1,700 per annum.

There is little information available about sole trader construction businesses and business failure. Anecdotally though, a high percentage of these businesses cease operating. The Australian Bureau of Statistics shows of the total 629,000 sole practitioner businesses in Australia existing in all industries in June 2018, only 54% were still around in June 2022 – an annual decline of 18.5%. Extrapolating these statistics to the national construction industry around 49,000 sole trader construction businesses cease operating every year, yet the awareness and attention is on the 1,700 company insolvencies.

But there are formal options available to sole trader and partnership businesses – though the best option is to act early.

Part IX Debt Agreement

In Australia the Bankruptcy Act provides people in financial difficulty a mechanism to reach an agreement with their creditors to release them from some of their debt.

To utilise Part IX the debtor (person owing money) must satisfy the following:

- have not been bankrupt in the previous 10 years, or a party to a Debt Agreement
- have unsecured debts that are below prescribed thresholds[43]
- have property that would be divisible among creditors in a bankruptcy that is below the threshold amount
- have a taxable income below the prescribed threshold.

Often businesses operated as sole trader businesses or partnerships have debts, property and income above the thresholds.

To enter into a Part IX Debt Agreement the debtor must put a proposal for a binding agreement, a statement of affairs and other evidence to the Official Receiver. The Official Receiver writes to creditors informing them of the proposal and provides the creditors with a summary of the debtor's statement of affairs. The Official Receiver asks the creditors whether the Debt Agreement should be accepted or whether a meeting of creditors should be called.

If the Debt Agreement proposal does not specify how the property is to be distributed, it must be distributed in proportion to provable debts. This provision only applies if there are insufficient funds to pay creditors in full.

The Debt Agreement only comes into effect when accepted by the creditors; 75% of creditors (in number and value) must resolve to accept the agreement for it to come into effect if a meeting is called, or 75% of creditors that reply if the proposal is processed in writing.

If a Debt Agreement is accepted by creditors the debtor is released from all remaining debts. Note the Debt Agreement only affects unsecured debts. Secured creditors rights are not impacted and personal guarantee obligations are not released via the Debt Agreement.

---

43 Thresholds are indexed. As at 2023 the threshold amounts were $133,278.60 for debts, $266,557.20 for property and $99,958.95 for income.

Part X Personal Insolvency Agreement

Like a Part IX Debt Agreement, a Part X Personal Insolvency Agreement is a more formal and more expensive agreement available to debtors in financial difficulty. The proposal can set out almost any lawful terms to pay some or all the debt owing, in a way and over a period that is agreed by both debtor and the creditors. For instance, it may contain the sale of some assets and a moratorium on creditor claims.

Unlike Part IX, the Part X provisions require the appointment of a Registered Trustee, or a solicitor, or the Official Trustee via an s188 authority. The Trustee will call a meeting of the creditors and take control of the debtor's property. Like in Part IX, the debtor needs to draft a Personal Insolvency Agreement (PIA) in the form of a deed and a statement of affairs.

The PIA must:

- identify the debtor's property that is to be available to pay creditors' claims
- identify the debtor's income that is to be available to pay creditors' claims
- specify the extent (if any) to which the debtor is to be released from his or her provable debts
- specify the conditions (if any) for the agreement to come into operation and the circumstances in which, or the events upon which, the agreement terminates
- specify the order in which proceeds of realising the property and/or income referred to in the agreement are to be distributed among creditors
- specify whether or not the Registered Trustee, or a solicitor, or the Official Trustee can pursue for the benefit of creditors any

transactions that have occurred prior to the day the agreement was executed

- make the provision for a nominated person or persons to be trustee or trustees of the agreement (and whether they will be paid, and if so, how they will be paid)
- provide that the debtor will execute such instruments and generally do all such acts and things in relation to his or her property and income as is required by the agreement.

Upon appointment of the trustee and until the meeting of creditors has decided whether to accept or reject the PIA, creditors are prevented from taking further action to recover the monies owed to them.

There are some advantages to entering into a PIA:

- the Trustee's appointment provides immediate independent control of the debtor's property and affairs
- the Trustee provides independent advice to creditors on the affairs of the debtor and the merits of the debtor's proposal
- the debtor avoids bankruptcy and the stigma associated with being bankrupt
- the PIA provides for the flexible administration of the debtor's affairs, including the opportunity to carry on business (this is extremely difficult to achieve for an undischarged bankrupt)
- there is an opportunity to obtain assets which are not available under bankruptcy
- the execution of a PIA avoids a court process in a creditor's bankruptcy petition
- subject to the terms of the PIA, there is no requirement to contribute property after the PIA is approved
- like a Part IX Debt Agreement, secured creditors' rights remain unaffected.

There are, however, some risks for the debtor:

- If the proposal for the PIA is not accepted by creditors, the most common outcome is for creditors to resolve that the debtor files for bankruptcy.
- The debtor may not have the funds to appoint and pay the Trustee.
- Credit agencies will be notified that a Trustee was appointed via the s188 authority.
- The debtor cannot act as a director of any company (including not-for-profit organisations or registered charities).
- Signing an s188 and various subsequent actions are acts of bankruptcy, and creditors can use this to apply to the court to have the debtor made bankrupt if the PIA is not accepted.
- The PIA attracts a 7% government charge, known as a realisation charge, which is payable before payments are paid to unsecured creditors.
- The PIA and the debtor's personal information are permanently on record in the National Personal Insolvency Index.

No Asset Procedure (New Zealand)

If you owe less than $50,000 (including secured debts but not non-provable debts) and are in New Zealand a No Asset Procedure (NAP) is probably the best formal insolvency solution. It lets you clear your debts and does not have the restrictions that bankruptcy does. It is only a 'one trick pony' though – once you have completed an NAP your only other insolvency option is bankruptcy.

To be eligible you must have no way to pay any of your debt and nothing you can sell to help make payments, including money in a bank or other funds. You cannot enter an NAP if a creditor intending to make you bankrupt would get a better result if you were made bankrupt, or if you have hidden assets. New Zealanders living overseas can enter an NAP – but be warned, the public register can be searched from overseas. Several credit reporting companies operate in more than one country so your credit rating outside of New Zealand may be affected. Creditors that are not based in New Zealand will also be sent a report if they are listed in your NAP, but they can continue to chase you for any money you owe them.

An NAP usually lasts for one year. When you enter the NAP, your debts are cleared. Your creditors do not get paid anything and they cannot continue chasing you for any debts included in your NAP.

By entered an NAP you confirm you have no realisable assets that could be sold to pay the debt. However, you are able to keep tools of trade, necessary household furniture (though a TV might not be considered necessary), a vehicle up to a threshold and a minimal amount of cash.

Your name would be published in the *New Zealand Gazette* as well as being recorded on the public register with the Insolvency and Trustee Service.

Debt Repayment Order (New Zealand)

A Debt Repayment Order (DRO), formerly known as Summary Instalment Order, is a good insolvency option if you owe less than $50,000 in unsecured debt and can make some repayments. A DRO gives you extra time to pay back some or all your debt – usually three years, though it can be more or less. You must be unable to pay off those debts right now but be able to make some repayments towards them over time.

A DRO is a formal repayment plan with your creditors. When applying for a DRO you are assigned a DRO supervisor who will work with all parties to arrange the details and the payment plan. While subject to a DRO you cannot take on any new debt over $1,000 without making the new creditor aware (in writing) that you are currently in a DRO. Once you've entered into a DRO, creditors cannot continue to chase you for payment of any unsecured debts included in the order or add any further penalties or interest to that debt.

A DRO is not advertised in a newspaper or the *New Zealand Gazette*, but it will be listed in the DRO Register with the Insolvency and Trustee Service.

Bankruptcy

Bankruptcy is a legal process whereby a Bankruptcy Trustee is appointed to manage an insolvent person's affairs and to provide a fair distribution of that person's divisible assets to their creditors.[44]

A person becomes bankrupt one of two ways: by initiating it themselves (a debtor's petition) or it being initiated by a creditor (creditor's petition).

A person must file a debtor's petition and a statement of affairs with the Australian Financial Security Authority or the New Zealand Insolvency and Trustee Service. A Trustee is then appointed to administer the bankruptcy by investigating the bankrupt's financial affairs and realising available assets to pay creditors.

With a creditor's petition, a creditor first applies to the court to make a judgement for their debts and serve a bankruptcy notice on the debtor. If the debt remains unpaid by the date on the bankruptcy notice the creditor may file a creditor's petition with the court seeking a 'sequestration order' and bankrupting the debtor.[45] A Trustee is appointed to administer the bankrupt's affairs.

The Trustee has the power to:

---

44 Not all of the bankrupt's assets are available to a bankruptcy trustee, such as items held in trust or loaned to the bankrupt. If they are not the bankrupt's assets they are not divisible assets.

45 A sequestration order is an order handed down by the court which makes you bankrupt.

- investigate the affairs of the bankrupt
- sell divisible property
- examine the bankrupt (and their associates) under oath
- manage and sell any of the bankrupt's businesses
- admit debts
- distribute dividends to creditors
- exercise the rights and powers the bankrupt had prior to them becoming bankrupt
- report to creditors
- report to regulators any offences of the bankrupt.

The bankrupt person is known as an 'undischarged bankrupt' from the date they are declared bankrupt until the bankruptcy is discharged or annulled. While in bankruptcy, a bankrupt:

- cannot be a company director
- cannot operate a registered business without advising people they are bankrupt (but can trade in their own name)
- must make available to the Trustee all their divisible assets
- must make available to the Trustee books, records and financial information, including those of associated entities such as companies and trusts
- must seek permission from the Trustee to travel overseas
- cannot obtain credit over a low threshold without informing the lender they are bankrupt.

A bankruptcy automatically ends three years (and one day) from when the bankruptcy is declared in Australia and New Zealand, though one year is being proposed. On discharge from bankruptcy, the bankrupt is released from most of the debts included in the bankruptcy and does not have to pay any more of the outstanding amount owed to the creditors included in the bankruptcy. However, the bankruptcy can be extended for up to eight years in Australia and five in New Zealand.

As with the Part X Personal Insolvency Agreement the bankruptcy status and personal information is permanently recorded on the National Personal Insolvency Index.

Income

While in bankruptcy the bankrupt is still able to earn income, however once past an annualised indexed threshold, part of the income must be paid to the Trustee. The Trustee will also assess this income level during the bankruptcy period.

Note also a bankrupt is not permitted to hold certain licences or positions; for example, directorships, building licences, liquor licences, financial services licences and real estate licences.

Assets

Divisible property when declared bankrupt is controlled by the Trustee. There are also some personal assets that the court will deem as non-divisible, including clothing and household items, tools of trade, vehicles to a prescribed value, life insurance policies, compensation payments, sentimental property and superannuation.

Any property acquired after being declared bankrupt is known as 'after-acquired property'. After-acquired property will vest with the Trustee, as soon as it is acquired by, or devolves on, the bankrupt. Examples are inheritances, lottery winnings and significant gifts.

Real property

Often the fear of losing the family home is a major impediment to someone declaring themselves bankrupt. There are different scenarios depending on the ownership structure of the property, the amount of equity in the property and the cooperation of the mortgagee.

If the property is solely in the bankrupt's name and unencumbered, it will be sold at market value by the Trustee. If the house is jointly owned the property moves to 'tenants in common' and the Trustee's name replaces that of the bankrupt. The Trustee will sell that share at market value, which may mean forcing a sale of the property. However, the Trustee commonly will work with the other owner/s to come up with an arrangement that is mutually beneficial. Often the bankrupt will have little or no equity in the property, and the Trustee has options to get a small return for creditors while enabling the bankrupt to retain possession or remain living in the property.

Discretionary (Family) Trusts

The Trustee can recover any property (such as cash, real estate or shares) that a bankrupt has given or sold to the trust at less than market value or that were moved to defeat creditors. The Trustee can also collect any monies owed to the bankrupt from the trust such as declared but unpaid distributions.

Tax refunds

Generally if the ATO or the Inland Revenue Department are a creditor of a bankrupt estate, any tax refunds during the bankruptcy period they can keep. After the bankruptcy is discharged, they cannot keep the refunds to pay the tax debts owed before bankruptcy.

Effects on creditors

Bankruptcy does not affect secured creditors' rights in relation to their security. For unsecured creditors, when a person is declared bankrupt their rights to claim the monies owed are exchanged with a right to receive a dividend or distribution from the Trustee. This only relates to provable debts. Non-provable debts such as student loans, court fines and unpaid maintenance payments cannot be claimed in bankruptcy and are also not released at the end of the bankruptcy (the bankrupt will still owe them at the end of the bankruptcy).

Bankruptcy in New Zealand

Bankruptcy in New Zealand is very similar to that in Australia. Notable differences though are:

- If you have debts of $1,000 or more a debtor to the Official Assignee or creditor petition can be lodged to begin the bankruptcy.

- If you have debts of more than $50,000, Debt Repayment Orders are not available to the debtor.

- Divisible property limits are different; for example, the vehicle value limit.

- The bankrupt cannot be employed by a relative or an entity controlled by a relative without permission of the Official Assignee.

- Breaking any rules of bankruptcy is a criminal offense.

- The bankrupt's name is published in their local paper and the *New Zealand Gazette*, as well as being recorded on the public register with the Insolvency and Trustee Service.

- If you are living overseas, you can still become bankrupt in New Zealand.

- Your retirement savings, including KiwiSaver, are an asset. However, in the case of a KiwiSaver scheme, the funds are protected from your creditors while they remain in the fund.

- You cannot apply for a new student loan until your bankruptcy is discharged or annulled.

* * *

There are some advantages to entering into bankruptcy:

- Any unsecured debts that remain unpaid will be written off at the end of the bankruptcy and any wage garnishment will cease.
- Creditors can no longer pursue you, the bankrupt, for payment and must deal with the Trustee.
- There is the possibility the bankrupt may be able to keep their home.
- The bankrupt can still earn an income.
- The bankrupt can keep necessary personal effects such as clothing, furniture and certain assets.
- Superannuation is generally protected.

There are also some disadvantages to entering into bankruptcy:

- The Trustee can sell the bankrupt's divisible assets.
- The bankrupt cannot act as a company director or officer or trade under an assumed name or registered business name without disclosure of bankruptcy.
- The bankrupt may lose licences; for example, builder's licence, real estate licence.
- The bankrupt must surrender their passport to the Trustee and can only travel overseas with the Trustee's permission.
- The bankrupt can only apply for credit up to an indexed amount, after which disclosure of the bankruptcy to creditors must be made.

- The bankrupt's credit rating will be affected.
- The bankrupt must surrender all financial books and records to the Trustee.

Composition proposal

In both Australia and New Zealand there is a legal avenue to have a bankruptcy annulled or cancelled. It is known as a 'composition' or 'arrangement' – the bankrupt offers and the creditors accept a proposal that is better than the dividend the creditors would receive if the bankruptcy runs its course.

To achieve the composition the bankrupt must secure further funds that can be made available to creditors. Typically, this is from a family member or wealthy benefactor. It can be for any amount and over any period.

The offer to creditors is made via the Trustee, and the bankrupt should discuss it with the Trustee before providing the final offer. The offer must also include the fees to the Trustee, and in Australia a 7% government realisation charge.

For the composition to be successful, 75% of creditors by value and numbers that attend the meeting of creditors must vote in favour of the composition.[46] If accepted, the bankruptcy is annulled and the 'ex bankrupt' and all creditors will be bound by the composition.

The bankrupt's name will appear on the public record National Personal Insolvency Index, with the record showing that the bankruptcy was annulled. Credit reporting businesses also keep records of bankruptcies for seven years.

---

46 Note the ATO and IRD are usually the biggest creditor by value. Not all compositions are accepted. There are often cases where the ATO and IRD do not accept a composition due to the compliance behaviour of the bankrupt, even though the composition gives a better outcome to all creditors.

Chapter 18

Creditor actions

Alternative Dispute Resolution

Alternative Dispute Resolution (ADR) is a dispute resolution process in Australia where an independent person (an ADR practitioner, such as a mediator) helps parties in dispute resolve their issues. ADR is a process that can be utilised before a dispute becomes so big that a court or tribunal is required to resolve the matter.

There are a range of ADR processes; for example, negotiation, mediation, arbitration, neutral evaluation, conciliation and an ombudsman. In each process there is an independent facilitator to assist both parties to resolve their dispute.

For disputes such as unpaid invoices, each state in Australia has a Small Business Commission (or similar). To find the right agency and process for your dispute the Australian Small Business and Family Enterprise Ombudsman website (https://asbfeo.gov.au) has a tool to identify the agency to contact.

Administrative tribunals

In each state in Australia there is an Administrative Tribunal; for example, the Victorian Civil & Administrative Tribunal (VCAT). One of their functions is to hear disputes relating to products and services bought or sold – trade disputes. You can also use the Tribunal to get an interim injunction.

Generally there is a timeframe of a few years to apply to the Tribunal to consider your claim.[47] To process the claim on the Civil Claims List, and then for both parties to provide the documentation can take three to four months. You can then expect to wait another eight to fourteen months for your case to be heard – so this is not a quick process. There is also a graduated application fee based on the value of the claim, and this could be as much as $2,500. In most instances you cannot be represented at the tribunal by lawyers though they can assist you to prepare for the Tribunal hearing.

The Tribunal has several actions available to it, including orders to make payment and garnishee notices. Failure to adhere to a Tribunal ruling can be used to commence other legal proceedings, such as a Statement of Claim.

Disputes Tribunal (NZ)

In New Zealand there is a similar process to the Administrative Tribunals in Australia known as the Disputes Tribunal. The Disputes Tribunal is inexpensive, flexible, quick, informal and private, and is used to resolve a range of disputes with claims under $30,000.[48] Like the Australian Administrative Tribunals there are no lawyers or

---

47 Generally, you must apply within six years of the dispute in Victoria, for example.

48 If a creditor brings a claim in the District Court for a disputed debt that's under $30,000, the Debtor can ask the court to transfer the case to the Disputes Tribunal by filing a notice of application for the transfer at the District Court.

judges in the Disputes Tribunal, with the focus more on what is fair and just rather than the points of law.

Disputes are heard by a Referee. Referees are appointed because of their personal qualities, knowledge and experience, and many referees have training in dispute resolution or have a law degree. The Referee works with the people on both sides of the dispute to see if they can reach an agreement. If they cannot agree, the Referee can make a binding decision.

Note the debt has to be disputed – undisputed debt claims cannot be pursued in the Disputes Tribunal but in either the District or High Court.[49]

Garnishee notices

A garnishee notice is a legal instrument or notice given to a third party of the debtor that has or will have monies owed by the debtor. For example, it may be the debtor's employer who is paying a wage or salary to the debtor, or a landlord that is in possession of a rental bond.

A garnishee notice can be issued to any person, business or organisation that:

- owes money, or will owe money to the debtor; or
- holds or will hold money on behalf of the debtor; or
- has or will have monies on account of another person, business or organisation for payment to the debtor; or
- has authority from some other person to pay the debtor.

Examples of who may receive a garnishee notice are employers, banks, landlords, real estate agents, insurers, the Tax Office and

---

49 District Court for debts less than $350,000 and High Court for amounts over $350,000.

companies that pay the debtor dividends. The types of payments that can be garnished are bank account interest, tax refunds, rental bonds, dividend payments and betting account payments.

When a third party receives a garnishee notice you, the debtor, will do so as well.[50]

To issue a garnishee notice the creditor usually seeks a court judgement or the ATO can issue a garnishee notice directly. This judgement allows the creditor to issue a court order that instructs the third party to redirect funds to the creditor.

Statutory demand

A statutory demand is a notice made by a creditor under the *Corporations Act 2001* on a debtor company (note the debtor must be a company and not a sole trader).

A statutory demand is a useful way to pressure a company to pay its debts. There is, however, a clear set of steps that must be followed:

- The debt must be for more than $2,000.
- The statutory demand must be on the prescribed form and accompanied by an affidavit verifying that the debt is due and payable.
- The court can set aside a demand if there is a genuine dispute or offsetting claim (and this is a low threshold). A caveat – only use the statutory demand if there is not a genuine dispute or else you may face indemnity costs.
- The service place for the demand is the registered office of the company being served. They have 21 days to apply for the demand to be set aside.

---

50 For companies, garnishee notices are sent to the directors. If sent from the ATO a copy is sent to your tax accountant.

Once a company receives a statutory demand, several things can happen:

- The debtor company pays the demand in full.
- The debtor company contacts the creditor company, and they negotiate a settlement.
- The debtor company applies to the court to have the demand set aside.
- The debtor company does not respond, and the creditor company applies to have the debtor company wound up.

A tip for all companies. Often companies (particularly smaller companies) are not very diligent at keeping their registered address up to date with ASIC, and I have seen this used by creditor companies really effectively.

I was working with a client who received a statutory demand that had been sent to their registered office. The client had 21 days to either apply for the demand to be set aside, pay the debt, negotiate a settlement or face being wound up.

The problem was they had not updated their registered office with ASIC and the statutory demand got sent to an address where they no longer had access to the mail.

Fortuitously, I was alerted to the demand, although it was after the 21-day period. My client had a genuine dispute but as the 21 days had passed, they were unable to apply to the court to set aside the demand. This left them two choices: pay the debt or be wound up. My client paid the debt, but this could have been avoided and, in fact, my client should have received money if they had only updated their registered address with ASIC.

Statement of claim

A statement of claim is the start of a court action and is the action of last resort. I would recommend you try the other methods that we have already discussed – one or some of them – before lodging a statement of claim.

A statement of claim is a form lodged at the Magistrates' Court that outlines a factual description of why you believe money is owed to you. There is a prescribed format, and you must include the date when the debt occurred, the place where the debt arose and a full and detailed description of the events that demonstrate why the money is owed, recorded in numbered paragraphs.

The statement of claim is then lodged at the court either nearest to where the claim arose or the defendant's address. There is a filing fee and a service fee that must be paid at the court.

So, what happens next? That depends on what the defendant does. They may:

- file a defence
- file an acknowledgment of liquidated claim
- do nothing – file nothing and pay nothing
- pay the total amount on the statement of claim
- pay an amount that is less than the total on the statement of claim
- file a cross-claim.

If the defendant files a defence form, it basically means they dispute your claim, and the case is headed to court as a defended case. There is a pre-trial review where both parties have an opportunity to settle.

Australian Taxation Office director penalty notices

The Australian Taxation Office has a special action for unpaid taxes it is owed by companies. It can issue a director penalty notice (DPN) that can make a director personally liable for Pay As You Go and Superannuation Guarantee Charge unpaid liabilities, and Goods and Services Tax (GST).

There are two types of director penalty notices:

- **21-Day or Remissible or Non-lockdown DPN:** The director has 21 days to make the company pay its ATO debts per the DPN or put the company into Voluntary Administration, liquidation or into the Small Business Restructuring Process. Note that the 21 days starts from when the ATO sends the DPN, not when the director receives it.

- **Lockdown DPN:** Issued to directors when they have failed to lodge the company's business activity statements (BAS), instalment statements (IAS) and/or SGC within three months of their due date.[51] The only option for the director is to pay the amounts in full. Putting the company into Voluntary Administration, liquidation or the Small Business Restructuring Process will not jettison the director's personal liability.

If a director becomes liable for ATO debts under a DPN, the ATO can use the range of actions above – for example, garnishee orders – to recover the monies. They can continue to pursue the director through to bankrupting them.

If one director pays the outstanding ATO debts, they have a 'right of indemnity' to pursue the other directors or the company.

---

51 Companies that use registered tax agents have another month.

Also note that Safe Harbour provisions only give directors some protection against insolvent trading claims and provisions and do not give protection from DPNs.

Getting help

Sources of help – Australia

Organisations to source help

- Byronvale Advisors
  https://byronvaleadvisors.com/
- Association of Business Restructuring and Turnaround
  https://abrt.org.au/
- Council of Small Business Organisations Australia
  https://www.cosboa.org.au/
- Turnaround Management Association Australia
  https://turnaround.org.au/
- Partners in Wellbeing
  https://www.partnersinwellbeing.org.au/small-business-support
- Small Business Debt Hotline
  https://sbdh.org.au/
- Small Business Association of Australia
  https://smallbusinessassociation.com.au/
- Family Business Australia
  https://www.familybusiness.org.au/
- Small Enterprise Association of Australia & New Zealand
  https://seaanz.org/
- INNOVIC
  https://www.innovic.com.au/
- Small Business Mentoring Service
  https://www.sbms.org.au/

Government organisations

- Business Victoria
  https://business.vic.gov.au/contact-us
- Business Tasmania
  https://www.business.tas.gov.au/home
- Service NSW
  https://www.service.nsw.gov.au/business/business-support
- Northern Territory Business Centres
  https://nt.gov.au/industry/business-support
- Small business WA
  https://www.smallbusiness.wa.gov.au/
- Small and Family Business SA
  https://business.sa.gov.au/
- Business Support ACT
  https://www.act.gov.au/business/business-support
- Department of Employment, Small Business and Training (Qld)
  https://desbt.qld.gov.au/small-business
- Business.gov.au
  https://business.gov.au/
- Victorian Small Business Commission
  https://www.vsbc.vic.gov.au/small-business-support/how-we-support-small-business/
- Fairwork Ombudsman
  https://smallbusiness.fairwork.gov.au/help-for-small-business
- Learn business workshops
  https://learn.business.vic.gov.au/
- Australian Small Business and Family Enterprise Ombudsman
  https://www.asbfeo.gov.au/my-business-health/home
- Rural Financial Counselling Service (RFCS)
  https://www.agriculture.gov.au/agriculture-land/farm-food-drought/drought/assistance/rural-financial-counselling-service

- Australian Taxation Office (ATO) Small Business Assist
  https://www.ato.gov.au/business/bus/supporting-your-small-business/
- Regional Development Australia
  https://www.rda.gov.au/

Dispute advice and advocacy

- Consumer Affairs Victoria
  https://www.consumer.vic.gov.au/
- Consumer Law Action Centre
  https://consumeraction.org.au/
- Law Action Victoria (LIV)
  https://www.liv.asn.au/find-a-lawyer
- Fair Trading NSW
  https://www.fairtrading.nsw.gov.au/buying-products-and-services/debt-collection,-repossession-of-goods-and-process-serving
- Business Queensland
  https://www.business.qld.gov.au/running-business/suppliers-stock/resolving-disputes#:~:text=The%20Queensland%20Small%20Business%20Commissioner,and%20retail%20shop%20lease%20disputes.
- Small Business Commission SA
  https://www.sasbc.sa.gov.au/disputes-and-mediation
- Department of Justice Tasmania
  https://www.justice.tas.gov.au/mediation_and_dispute_resolution
- Small Business WA
  https://www.smallbusiness.wa.gov.au/dispute-resolution
- Access ACT
  https://www.accesscanberra.act.gov.au/s/services/consumer-complaint

- NT.GOV.AU
  https://nt.gov.au/law/rights/dispute-with-a-business/dispute-resolution

Banks and lender support

- Commonwealth Bank of Australia
  https://www.commbank.com.au/business/small-business.html
- National Australia Bank
  https://www.nab.com.au/contact-us/business/financial-hardship-support
- Australian Banking Association
  https://www.ausbanking.org.au/for-customers/financial-difficulty/
- ANZ Bank Customer Connect
  https://www.anz.com.au/support/financial-hardship/
- Westpac Assist
  https://www.westpac.com.au/about-westpac/sustainability/initiatives-for-you/customers-financial-hardship/

Business owner health resources

- Beyond Blue
  https://www.beyondblue.org.au/get-support/newaccess-mental-health-coaching
- My Business Health
  https://www.asbfeo.gov.au/my-business-health/home
- Lifeline
  https://www.lifeline.org.au/
- MensLine
  https://www.lifeline.org.au/
- Heads up
  https:// www.headsup.org

- Suicide Call Back Service
  https://www.suicidecallbackservice.org.au/
- The Mentally Healthy Workplace Alliance
  https://mentallyhealthyworkplacealliance.org.au/
- Counting on U
  https://blogs.deakin.edu.au/counting-on-u/
- Mental Health First Aid Australia
  https://mhfa.com.au/mhfa-workplace
- RU OK
  https://www.ruok.org.au/work
- TIACS (This is a Conversation Starter)
  https://www.tiacs.org/

Sources of help – New Zealand

Organisations to source help

- Byronvale Advisors
  https://byronvaleadvisors.com/
- Small Business New Zealand
  https://www.sbnz.co.nz/
- New Zealand Chambers of Commerce
  https://www.newzealandchambers.co.nz/
- Small Enterprise Association of Australia & New Zealand
  https://seaanz.org/
- MoneyTalks
  https://www.moneytalks.co.nz/home/
- Good Shepherd
  https://goodshepherd.org.nz/
- Sorted
  https://sorted.org.nz/

- Citizens Advice Bureau
  https://www.cab.org.nz/
- Spring
  https://www.spring.kiwi/
- Business Mentors New Zealand
  https://www.businessmentors.org.nz/
- Co.OFWomen
  https://coofwomen.biz/

Government organisations

- Ministry of Business, Innovation & Employment
  Hikina Whakatutuki
  https://www.mbie.govt.nz/business-and-employment/business/
  support-for-business/
- Business.govt.nz
  https://www.business.govt.nz/
- Connected
  https://www.connected.govt.nz/support-for-business/
- New Zealand Trade & Enterprise *Te Taurapa Tuhono*
  https://my.nzte.govt.nz/

Banks and lender support

- Westpac New Zealand
  https://www.westpac.co.nz/business/tools-rates-fees/
  business-base/
- ASB Bank
  https://www.asb.co.nz/business-banking?fm=footer:link:
  business
- ANZ Bank
  https://www.anz.co.nz/business/

- Bank of New Zealand
  https://www.bnz.co.nz/contact/financial-concerns/
  experiencing-financial-difficulty/
- New Zealand Investment Network
  https://www.newzealandinvestmentnetwork.co.nz/
  business-funding

Dispute advice and advocacy

- Government Centre for Dispute Resolution
  https://www.mbie.govt.nz/cross-government-functions/
  government-centre-for-dispute-resolution/
- New Zealand Dispute Resolution Centre
  Te Pokapu Whatakau o Aotearoa
  https://nzdrc.co.nz/
- Arbitrators' and Mediators' Institute of New Zealand Inc
  Te Mana Kaiwhakatau, Takawaenga o Aotearoa
  https://www.aminz.org.nz/
- Disputes Tribunal of New Zealand
  https://www.disputestribunal.govt.nz/
- The Centre for Alternative Dispute Resolution
  Te Whakatau Tautohe Haurahi Ke
  https://adrcentre.co.nz/

Business owner health resources

- First Steps Nga Hihoi Tuatahi
  https://firststeps.nz/
- Business Leaders' Health & Safety Forum
  https://www.forum.org.nz/resources/
- Worksafe Mahi Haumaru Aotearoa
  https://www.worksafe.govt.nz/topic-and-industry/work-
  related-health/mental-health/

- Business.govt.nz
  https://www.business.govt.nz/wellbeing-support/wellbeing-in-your-business/mental-health-workplace/
- Be Brave in Business e-learning series
  https://www.business.govt.nz/wellbeing-support/brave-in-business-e-learning/

The Babel fish

'If you stick a Babel fish in your ear you can instantly understand anything said to you in any form of language.'

Douglas Adams

3-statement forecast – a forecasting tool that integrates the Balance Sheet, Profit and Loss Statement and Cashflow Statement in a dynamic way so the user can see the impact on decisions and different scenarios.

ASIC – Australian Securities and Investments Commission – an independent Australian Government body set up under and administering the *Australian Securities and Investments Commission Act 2001* (ASIC Act), and carry out most of their work under the Corporations Act.

ATO – Australian Taxation Office – not the fifth bank!

Balance sheet solvency test – compares the current or realisable assets against current liabilities, and if liabilities are greater than assets the business fails the solvency test.

Bankruptcy – a legal process where a bankruptcy trustee is appointed to manage an insolvent person's affairs, and to provide a fair distribution of that person's divisible assets to their creditors.

Boiled frog – businesses have characteristics of introversion and inertia in the face of business environmental change.

Bullfrogs – are expensive show-offs that need to be seen with all the trappings of success, status and power.

Cashflow – the movement of money in and out of the business.

Cashflow solvency test – also known as the commercial solvency test, it looks at whether a business can pay its liabilities as and when they fall due.

Cash rationing – is a process to decide how to allocate cash to different areas or projects of the business, given the limited amount of cash available.

Cash-to-cash cycle – a measure of the time from purchase of materials, products and supplies to the time of the receipt of cash from the sale of those material, products or supplies.

Consignment – an arrangement where the purchaser, also referred to as a consignee, agrees to pay a seller, or consignor, for merchandise after the item sells. Common in retail businesses – books such as this are usually sold to bookshops on consignment.

Cost of Goods Sold (COGS) – the cost of directly producing the goods sold.

Creditors – people and businesses you owe money to.

Creditor Days – average time from purchase to payment of goods and services.

Current assets – cash and other assets that are expected to be converted to cash within a year; for example, accounts receivable, inventory, prepayments.

Current liabilities – short-term financial obligations that are due within one year; for example, accounts payable, accrued expenses, GST, payroll taxes, superannuation payable, interest.

Debtors – people and businesses that owe you money.

Debtor Days – average time from sale to receiving payment.

Decentralisation – breaking the business into smaller units with managers directly having accountability for those units.

Drowned frog leader – an overambitious, super-salesperson type who is so set on hyper-successful performance that he or she ceases to believe in the existence of failure.

Factoring – a type of financing where the debt, and the responsibility for collecting that debt is 'sold' to a finance company. The finance company would pay the seller of the debt straight away, less commissions and interest.

Garnishee notice – a legal instrument or notice given to a third party of the debtor that has or will have monies owed to the debtor.

Goldfish memory syndrome – an expression describing a situation that somebody easily loses their train of thought and forgets things.

Hardcore – inventory that has been written off in accounting but still physically exists. May or may not be obsolete.

Inland Revenue Department – New Zealand's taxation department (Te Tari Taake Department).

Insolvent – means the business is unable to pay its debts as and when they fall due.

IRD – New Zealand Inland Revenue Department

Kawdigoo – an Inuit word meaning *the water has settled clear* – when life gets tangled you follow the river until the chaos falls away.

Leakage – the wastage of time, effort, cash or materials.

Leadership – a set of behaviours used to help people align their collective direction, to execute strategic plans, and to continually renew their business.

Liquidity – how much cash could your business access if you had to pay off what you owe today —and how fast could you get it?

Management buy-in (MBI) – is a corporate action in which an outside manager or management team purchases a controlling ownership stake in an outside company and replaces its existing management team.

Non-provable debts – debts such as student loans, court imposed fines, maintenance payments, personal clothing and household items, tools of trade.

'Oh my god we killed Kenny!' syndrome – also known as 'blue-bottle syndrome' in discussing stress management. It describes an environment whereby people can only operate in total chaos.

Organisational change – the is the process of moving from established to new ways of thinking, behaving or working.

Opportunity cost – the value you lose by choosing one alternative over another.

Ostrich syndrome – a cognitive bias where people tend to 'bury their head in the sand' and avoid potentially negative but useful information.

Payables – creditors – people and businesses you owe money to.

Phoenix company – a company that 'rises from the ashes' of a failed or insolvent company.

Polymath – an individual whose knowledge spans a substantial number of subjects, known to draw on complex bodies of knowledge to solve specific problems.

Pre-pack arrangement – a legally binding agreement to rescue an insolvent business before the formal appointment of an insolvency practitioner. It is a sale process where the business assets, or the whole business, is sold prior to the appointment of an insolvency practitioner. The insolvency practitioner would review the sale terms and if appropriate ratify the sale agreement.

Receivables – debtors – people and businesses that owe you money.

Safe Harbour – a provision under the Corporations Act in Australia that allows some relief against a director's duty to prevent a company trading while insolvent.

SMEs – small and medium-sized enterprises.

Standstill agreement – a formal agreement between the business and the funder whereby the parties agree to stand limitation periods still – allowing the business time without legal action being taken against them, or current action is halted, to restructure.

Statement of Claim – a document filed with the court that summarises the facts regarding the monies owed by the debtor to the creditor.

Strategic drift – is a business's failure to recognise and respond to changes within its business environment.

Sunk costs – costs that have occurred in the past that can no longer be controlled or managed such as patents, the cost of incorporation, and research and development.

SWOT analysis – an analysis of the business's strengths, weaknesses, opportunities and threats.

Tadpoles – are either failed startups, or in large business settings are an established business brought down by a failed big new project or product.

Voluntary Administration – a formal insolvency process where the directors of an insolvent company appoint an administrator.

VUCA – Volatility, uncertainty, complexity and ambiguity. A US Army War College leadership concept.

Working capital – the difference between current assets and current liabilities. It is a measure of a business's liquidity – the ability to pay its bills that are due and unexpected debts.

Zero-based budgeting – or ZBB, is a technique where a budget is formed with no regard to previous budgets or performance – it starts from a zero base, i.e., from scratch, and is not based on previous trends.

Acknowledgements

Thank you to the people in the turnaround and insolvency community that provided encouragement to write this book. Without this it would never have been finished and remained a collection of my thoughts on a computer. I would especially like to call out from this cohort Eddie Griffith from the Association of Business Restructuring and Turnaround.

Thank you to my clients – the true heroes who have tried, failed, stood back up, and learned from their mistakes, and worked hard to turn their businesses around. I would especially acknowledge Andy[52] for allowing me to use his case and business in many of the examples and anecdotes in this book. After a tough couple of years and his tireless effort, he has not only turned the business around but grown it to four times the size. Providing the help and support, and then seeing businesses flourish inspires and motivates me more than anything to keep working with distressed businesses.

Michael, Anna and the entire team at Publish Central for helping get the book edited, formatted, designed and printed.

Liz, Laura and Amy – my family – thank you for just being you and letting me do 'my thing'.

---

52 Andy is a real client, but as with most of my clients there is a stigma associated with business failure, so no surname or identifying information has been provided to protect and respect his privacy.

About the author

Stephen has been advising businesses for over 30 years – from very small, sole trader businesses through to large multinationals, and everything in between. It is more than a job to Stephen – it is a passion. Success to Stephen (and yes, enjoyment) is helping a business survive, become sustainable and prosper. He is very mindful that a business is about people and each stakeholder is a person. He understands that business owners not only have a financial responsibility, but they are accountable and responsible to people – employees, their own family, suppliers (and their employees and families), banks, landlords, the local community and more. This is what keeps Stephen awake at night during a turnaround – the impact and the ramifications of actions, or inactions, on other people.

For a number of years Stephen has been running his firm Byronvale Advisors – turnaround and crisis management advisors. He also has a small investment firm Byronvale Angel Investments that invests only in businesses in distress or crisis.

Outside of work, Stephen is a husband to Liz and is the father of two teenage daughters, Laura and Amy. When time permits, he enjoys getting some 'Zen time', usually out on a river flyfishing, in the garden, or making things in his workshop.

This is Stephen's second business book. His first book *Run Your Business Better* was published in July 2017. It was written for small businesses and sole traders – who are usually very good at what they do, but often lack the skills, and time, to run their business well.[53]

---

53 Stephen has also ghost-written a book for a client.

References

Aitken Whyte Lawyers. (2023). *Determining Solvency of a Company – Cash Flow Assessment Confirmed as the Most Appropriate Method.* Retrieved from Aitken Whyte Lawyers: https://www.awbrisbanelawyers.com.au/determining-solvency-of-company-cash-flow-assessment-wound-up-in-insolvency-corporations-act/

Alcock, D. (2022, July 1). *Signs and indicators of insolvency.* Retrieved from Worrells: https://worrells.net.au/resources/news/signs-and-indicators-of-insolvency

Alexander, N. (2019, February 4). *The Top 10 every turnaround leader must have (part 1).* Retrieved from LinkedIn: https://www.linkedin.com/pulse/top-10-every-turnaround-leader-must-have-part-1-nick-alexander/

Alonso, T. (2022, November 3). *Strategic Drift: How to avoid losing competitive advantage.* Retrieved from Cascade: https://www.cascade.app/blog/strategic-drift

Angwin, D., Sammut-Bonnici, T., & McGee, J. (2015, January). *Turnaround Strategy.* Retrieved from ResearchGate.

Australian Financial Security Authority. (2023). *Am I eligible for a debt agreement?* Retrieved from Australian Financial Security Authority: https://www.afsa.gov.au/i-cant-pay-my-debts/debt-agreement/am-i-eligible-debt-agreement

Australian Financial Security Authority. (2023). *What is a debt agreement?* Retrieved from https://www.afsa.gov.au/i-cant-pay-my-debts/debt-agreement/what-debt-agreement

Australian Government Attorney-General's Department. (2014, January 22). *Your Guide to Dispute Resolution.* Retrieved from Australian Government Attorney-General's Department: https://www.ag.gov.au/legal-system/publications/your-guide-dispute-resolution

Australian Securities & Investment Commission. (2023). *Insolvency for directors.* Retrieved from Australian Securities & Investment Commission: https://asic.gov.au/regulatory-resources/insolvency/insolvency-for-directors/

Australian Securities & Investment Commission. (n.d.). *Restructuring and the restructuring plan.* Retrieved from https://asic.gov.au/regulatory-resources/insolvency/insolvency-for-directors/restructuring-and-the-restructuring-plan/

Ayiecha, F. O., & Katuse, P. (2014, March). Implementing Turnaround Strategy: Effect of Change Management and Management Competence factors. *IOSR Journal of Business and Management, 16*(3), 95-103.

Bain & Company. (2023, January 31). *Zero-Based Budgeting.* Retrieved from Bain & Company: https://www.bain.com/insights/management-tools-zero-based-budgeting/

Bain & Company. (2023). *Zero-based Budgeting (ZBB).* Retrieved from Bain & Company: https://www.bain.com/consulting-services/performance-improvement/zero-based-budgeting/

Baker, H. (2021, February 22). *6 most commonly overlooked cost savings in business.* Retrieved from Dynamic Business: https://dynamicbusiness.com/leadership-2/business-cost-savings-tips-advice-2021.html

Balasubramanian, S., & Fernandes, C. (2022, January 10). Confirmation of a crisis leadership model and its effectiveness: Lessons from the COVID-19 pandemic. *Cogent Business & Management, 9*(1).

Bankruptcy and Houses | How does Personal Bankruptcy impact the family home? (2023). *Bankruptcy and Houses | How does Personal Bankruptcy impact the family home?* Retrieved from Rapsey Griffiths: https://rapseygriffiths.com.au/bankruptcy-and-houses-how-does-personal-bankruptcy-impact-the-family-home/

BDO Australia. (2022, August 02). *When was the last time you prepared a three-way forecast?* Retrieved from BDO Australia: https://www.bdo.com.au/en-au/insights/advisory/articles/when-was-the-last-time-you-prepared-a-three-way-forecast

Bizshifts-Trends. (2018, May 13). Retrieved from https://bizshifts-trends.com/triage-in-business-resilience-to-survive-crippling-disaster-process-that-calls-for-swift-prioritized-actions/

Blaney, M. (2002). *Turning a Business Around, 2nd edition.* How To Books.

Bohm, W. (2019, January 3). Zero-based budgeting gets a second look. (McKinsey-on-Finance, Interviewer)

Bort, J. (2023, April 24). *WeWork has frittered away $46.7 billion in value as the stock sinks below 50 cents, one of the biggest startup failures of all time, and venture capitalists haven't learned a thing.* Retrieved from Insider: https://www-businessinsider-com.cdn.ampproject.org/c/s/www.businessinsider.com/wework-startup-failure-benchmark-insight-partners-venture-capitalists-learned-nothing-2023-4?amp

Brinded, T., Kok, E., Lucas, P., & Watson, B. (2022, June 29). *How capital expenditure management can drive performance.* Retrieved from McKinsey & Company: https://www.mckinsey.com/capabilities/strategy-and-corporate-finance/our-insights/how-capital-expenditure-management-can-drive-performance

Buchanan, R. (2019, November 11). *Understanding turnaround leadership in business.* University of Pretoria, Gordon Institute of Business Science.

Business Jargons. (2023). *Turnaround Strategy.* Retrieved from Business Jargons: https://businessjargons.com/turnaround-strategy.html

Butler, S. (2022, March 9). *Director penalty notices: payment arrangements no longer part of the plan.* Retrieved from Hall& Wilcox: https://hallandwilcox.com.au/thinking/director-penalty-notices-payment-arrangements-no-longer-part-of-the-plan/

Cantone, D. (2023). *Role of the new small business restructuring practitioner (SBRP).* Retrieved from Oracle: https://oracleis.com.au/role-of-the-new-small-business-restructuring-practitioner-sbrp/

CFI Team. (2020, July 29). *Turnaround Recovery Strategies.* Retrieved from Corporate Finance Institute: https://corporatefinanceinstitute.com/resources/management/turnaround-recovery-strategies/

Chartered Accountants Australia New Zealand. (2023). *Insolvency and restructuring.* Retrieved from https://www.charteredaccountantsanz.com/member-services/technical/insolvency-and-restructuring

Community Law. (2023). *How debts are recovered through the courts.* Retrieved from Community Law: https://communitylaw.org.nz/community-law-manual/chapter-26-credit-and-debt/guarantors/how-debts-are-recovered-through-the-courts/

Community Law. (2023). *Overview of the Disputes Tribunal.* Retrieved from Community Law: https://communitylaw.org.nz/community-law-manual/chapter-6-the-disputes-tribunal/overview-of-the-disputes-tribunal/

Cook, C. (2014, October 1). *Business survival impossible without the support of critical stakeholders*. Retrieved from Worrells: https://worrells.net.au/resources/news/business-survival-impossible-without-the-support-of-critical-stakeholders

Davies, R., Kinet, L., & Lo, B. (2015, April 1). *Can we talk? Five tips for communicating in turnarounds*. Retrieved from McKinsey & Company: https://www.mckinsey.com/capabilities/strategy-and-corporate-finance/our-insights/can-we-talk-five-tips-for-communicating-in-turnarounds#/

Dissolve. (2018). *What is a Phoenix Company?* Retrieved from https://www.dissolve.com.au/information-centre/what-is-a-phoenix-company/

Dobbie, P. (2021). The 10 Guiding Principles To Successful Turnarounds [Recorded by M. Fingland]. Retrieved from Vantage Performance: https://www.vantageperformance.com.au/10-guiding-principles-successful-turnarounds/

DPN Solutions. (2023). *Received a Director Penalty Notice?* Retrieved from DPN Solutions: https://www.dpnsolutions.com.au/

DW Consulting. (2023). *Turnaround Consulting*. Retrieved from DW Consulting: https://www.dwadvisory.com.au/services/turn-around-advisory-index/turn-around-advisory/21-turnaround-consulting?Itemid=150

Eby, K. (2019, February 15). *Quality Improvement Processes: The Basics and Beyond*. Retrieved from Smartsheet: https://www.smartsheet.com/quality-improvement-process

Eskhill. (2022). *Frog @ Eskhill*. Retrieved from Eskhill: https://www.eskhill.com/frog.htm

Fernando, J. (2023, March 27). *Inventory Turnover Ratio: What It Is, How It Works, and Formula*. Retrieved from Investopedia: https://www.investopedia.com/terms/i/inventoryturnover.asp

Fingland, M. (2017). Ten reasons why leaders don't seek help with their business. (P. Dobbie, Interviewer) Retrieved from Vantage Performance.

Fingland, M. (2020, November 5). *The critical role of a Chief Restructuring Officer - Turnaround Tips with Michael Fingland*. Retrieved from Vantage Performance: https://www.youtube.com/watch?v=-M-qN45TV3I

Fingland, M. (2021, March 29). *Beware the Rapid Growth Trap - Turnaround Tips with Michael Fingland*. Retrieved from Vantage Performance: https://www.youtube.com/watch?v=X9N36Yfe-2I

Fingland, M. (2021, October 29). *Turnaround Tips*. Retrieved from Vantage Performance: https://www.youtube.com/watch?v=T7wSIMEhW7k

Fingland, M. (2021, March 29). *What does a turnaround advisor actually do? - Turnaround Tips with Michael Fingland*. Retrieved from Vantage Performance: https://www.youtube.com/watch?v=nHB6N85OzYw

Fingland, M. (2023, April). *Early Intervention - The Holy Grail of Turnaround*. Retrieved from LinkedIn: https://www.linkedin.com/posts/michael-fingland-34a09b3_early-intervention-the-holy-grail-of-turnaround-activity-7054242193049350144-K3HW/?utm_source=share&utm_medium=member_ios

Fingland, M. (2023). *Financial Restructuring in a Turnaround Context*. Retrieved from Vantage Performance: https://www.vantageperformance.com.au/financial-restructuring-in-turnaround/

Fingland, M. (2023, May 15). *Managing Your Business Through A Downturn*. Retrieved from https://www.linkedin.com/pulse/managing-your-business-through-downturn-michael-fingland/

Fingland, M. (2023, May). *The art of developing a cash runway in a turnaround.* Retrieved from LinkedIn: https://www.linkedin.com/posts/michael-fingland-34a09b3_the-art-of-developing-a-cash-runway-in-a-activity-7059678014720151553-ZG_j/?utm_source=share&utm_medium=member_ios

Fingland, M. (2023). *Why Communication Matters in a Turnaround.* Retrieved from Vantage Performance: https://vantageperformance.com.au/why-communication-matters-in-a-turnaround/

Gammel, C. D. (2020, July 14). *A New Era of Leadership: The Turnaround CEO.* Retrieved from McKinley Advisors: https://www.mckinley-advisors.com/blog/a-new-era-of-leadership-the-turnaround-ceo

Grant, D. (2023). *Solvent or Insolvent? Principles applied by the Courts to determine solvency of a company.* Retrieved from Boss Lawyers: https://www.bosslawyers.com.au/solvent-or-insolvent-principles-applied-by-the-courts-to-determine-solvency-of-a-company/

Grégoire, P. (2022, June 10). *Stakeholder Mapping: When, Why, and How to Map Stakeholders.* Retrieved from Borealis: https://www.boreal-is.com/blog/stakeholder-mapping-identify-stakeholders/

Hans. (2023). *7 Proven Business Turnaround Strategy Steps.* Retrieved from The Business Sniper: https://thebusinesssniper.com/turnaround-strategy-steps/

Hargovan, A. (2023). *Putting assets beyond the reach of creditors: An audacious example of illegal phoenixing and its legal implications.* Retrieved from Governance Institute of Australia: https://www.governanceinstitute.com.au/resources/governance-directions/volume-74-number-6/putting-assets-beyond-the-reach-of-creditors-an-audacious-example-of-illegal-phoenixing-and-its-legal-implications/?_cldee=qks2cQw58McXT29mS3Ki5oxqdumosAT2x3Y-G_ezDW

Harris, J. (2020, October 9). *A New System for SME Restructuring: Is there a business doctor in the house?* Retrieved from Australian Insolvency Law: https://australianinsolvencylaw.com/2020/10/09/a-new-system-for-sme-restructuring/

Houston, M. (2020, October 8). *5 Ways Financial Mismanagement Will Kill Your Business.* Retrieved from Forbes: https://www.forbes.com/sites/melissahouston/2020/10/08/5-ways-financial-mismanagement-will-kill-your-business/?sh=6328740b3001

Hyde, J., & Koumalats, K. (2021, March 4). *4 Characteristics of an Effective Turnaround Leader.* Retrieved from Region 13: https://blog.esc13.net/4-characteristics-of-an-effective-turnaround-leader/

Indeed. (2023, February 4). *How To Improve Operational Efficiency in 5 Steps (With Tips).* Retrieved from Indeed: https://www.indeed.com/career-advice/career-development/how-to-improve-operational-efficiency

Institute for Management Development. (2022, August). *What is situational leadership?* Retrieved from IMD: https://www.imd.org/reflections/situational-leadership/

Interimexecs. (2023). *Maximizing Operational Efficiency: Expert COOs Offer Tips for Improving Process and Productivity.* Retrieved from Interimexecs: https://interimexecs.com/maximizing-operational-efficiency-expert-coos-offer-tips-for-improving-processes-and-productivity/

Kanter, R. M. (2003, June). *Leadership and the Psychology of Turnarounds.* Retrieved from Harvard Business Review: https://hbr.org/2003/06/leadership-and-the-psychology-of-turnarounds

Kaufman, J. (2012). *The Personal MBA*. London: Penguin Group.

Kaye, T. (2018, November 23). *Are you invested in an ASX zombie?* Retrieved from https://www.eurekareport.com.au/: https://www.eurekareport.com.au/investment-news/are-you-invested-in-an-asx-zombie/144035

Kenton, W. (2021, May 21). *Management Buy-In: Everything to Know About MBI*. Retrieved from Investopedia: https://www.investopedia.com/terms/m/mbi.asp

Lander & Rogers. (2017, August). *The conflict of potential administrators becoming administrators — Ten Network Holdings*. Retrieved from https://www.landers.com.au/legal-insights-news/the-conflict-of-potential-administrators-becoming-administrators-ten-network-holdings

LawRight. (2023). *Commencing court proceedings*. Retrieved from LawRight: https://www.lawright.org.au/legal-information/going-to-court/commencing-court-proceedings/

Levy, S. (2022, July 8). *How Hemingway Gradually Then suddenly Defined the Zeitgeist*. Retrieved from Wired: https://www.wired.com/story/plaintext-hemingway-gradually-suddenly-zeitgeist/

LinkedIn. (2023). *How do you leverage stakeholder support and collaboration to accelerate the turnaround process and outcomes?* Retrieved from LinkedIn: https://www.linkedin.com/advice/0/how-do-you-leverage-stakeholder-support

Martin, S. (2020, December 14). Retrieved from Center for Creative Leadership: https://www.ccl.org/articles/leading-effectively-articles/communicating-in-a-crisis-what-when-and-how/

McKinsey & Company. (2022, August 17). *What is leadership?* Retrieved from McKinsey & Company: https://www.mckinsey.com/featured-insights/mckinsey-explainers/what-is-leadership

Merriam-Webster Online Dictionary. (2020). Retrieved from https://www.merriam-webster.com/dictionary/triage

Mind Tools. (2023). *Stakeholder Analysis*. Retrieved from Mind Tools: https://www.mindtools.com/aolorms/stakeholder-analysis

Mind Tools. (2023). *Turnaround Management*. Retrieved from MindTools: https://www.mindtools.com/aw6ls66/turnaround-management

Mind Tools Content Team. (2023). *Managing in a VUCA World*. Retrieved from Mind Tools: https://www.mindtools.com/asnydwg/managing-in-a-vuca-world

Money Hub. (2021, June 9). *Bankruptcy in New Zealand - The Definitive Guide*. Retrieved from https://www.moneyhub.co.nz/bankruptcy.html

Moore, F. C., & Obradovich, N. (2019, February 25). Retrieved from The Washington Post: https://www.washingtonpost.com/weather/2019/02/25/data-are-frogs-dont-boil-we-might/

Morris, R. A. (2004, May). Retrieved from American Bankruptcy Institute: https://www.abi.org/abi-journal/turnaround-or-restructuring

Muncey, J. (2023, May 11). *What's the Purpose of a Statement of Claim?* Retrieved from LegalVision: https://legalvision.com.au/whats-the-purpose-of-a-statement-of-claim/

Needs, J. (2023, July 14). *Almost half of Kiwi small business owners unable to pay themselves*. Retrieved from Accounting Times: https://www.accountingtimes.com.au/profession/almost-half-of-kiwi-small-business-owners-unable-to-pay-themselves

New Zealand Insolvency and Trustee Service. (2023). *Bankruptcy*. Retrieved from New Zealand Insolvency and Trustee Service: https://www.insolvency.govt.nz/personal-debt/personal-insolvency-options/bankruptcy/

Norcross, J., Prochaska, J., & DiClemente, C. (1994). *Changing for Good*. HarperCollins Publishers Inc.

Nyatsunba, K. M., & Pooe, D. (2021, August 17). *Failure to implement a turnaround strategy at South African Airways: Reflections from strategic players*. Retrieved from Taylor & Francis Online: https://www.tandfonline.com/doi/full/10.1080/0376835X.2021.1965865

O'Brien Palmer Insolvency & Business Advisory. (2014). *Part X Personal Insolvency Agreement ('PIA')*. Retrieved from https://obp.com.au/part-x-personal-insolvency-agreement/

Oracle. (2023). *What is zero-based budgeting (ZBB)?* Retrieved from Oracle: https://www.oracle.com/au/performance-management/planning/zero-based-budgeting/

Otway, S. (2023). *Loan Accounts*. Retrieved from SV Partners: https://svpartners.com.au/loan-accounts/

Papadopoulos, J. (2020, November 10). *What is a garnishee order and how can you stop it?* Retrieved from Canstar: https://www.canstar.com.au/credit-score/what-is-a-garnishee-order/

Paul Apathy, M. C. (2022, July 20). *Safe Harbour Protections May Help Australian Startups & Scaleups Ride Out The Current Storm*. Retrieved from Herbert Smith Freehills: https://www.mondaq.com/australia/insolvencybankruptcy/1213930/safe-harbour-protections-may-help-australian-startups-scaleups-ride-out-the-current-storm

Pearce & Heers. (2023). *Small Business Restructuring: What are the problems and risks*. Retrieved from https://pearceheers.com.au/small-business-restructuring-what-are-the-problems-and-risks/

Pitcher Partners. (2017). Business Recovery and Insolvency. *Guide to our services*.

Price, J. (2020, October 21). *The decline & recovery curve – Why early action is key!* Retrieved from Turpin Baker Armstrong Insolvency: https://www.turpinbainsolvency.co.uk/blog/decline-recovery-curve

Proctor, J. (2012, September 25). *Business Transformation: Business Process Reengineering vs. Corporate Turnaround*. Retrieved from Inteqgroup: https://www.inteqgroup.com/blog/business-process-reengineering-vs-business-turnaround

Prophix. (2021, September 2). *Zero-Based Budgeting or Rolling Forecasts? Can Finance do Both?* Retrieved from Prophix: https://blog.prophix.com/zero-based-budgeting-or-rolling-forecasts-can-finance-do-both/

Rapaport, E. (2020, April 15). *how-to-spot-a-company-in-financial-distress*. Retrieved from Morningstar: https://www.morningstar.com.au/stocks/article/how-to-spot-a-company-in-financial-distress-/201477

Rapsey Griffiths. (2022, April 13). *7 Strategies of turnaround – Financial restructuring (Part 7 of 7)*. Retrieved from Rapsey Griffiths: https://rapseygriffiths.com.au/7-strategies-of-turnaround-financial-restructuring-part-7-of-7/

Rapsey Griffiths. (2022, March 15). *7 strategies of turnaround – Stakeholder support (Part 3 of 7)*. Retrieved from Rapsey Griffiths: https://rapseygriffiths.com.au/7-strategies-for-turnaround-leadership-cuts-and-reshuffling-part-3-of-7/

Rapsey Griffiths. (2023). *10 Early warning signs that you need a business turnaround*. Retrieved from Rapsey Griffiths: https://rapseygriffiths.com.au/business-turnaround-10-early-warning-signs/

Rapsey Griffiths. (2023). *1-year bankruptcy*. Retrieved from Rapsey Griffiths: https://rapseygriffiths.com.au/1-year-bankruptcy/

Rapsey Griffiths. (2023). *4 ways to get rid of your debt and get on with your life.* Retrieved from Rapsey Griffiths: https://rapseygriffiths.com.au/4-ways-to-get-rid-of-your-debt/

Rapsey Griffiths. (2023). *4 ways to help your clients avoid tax debts on their credit report.* Retrieved from Rapsey Griffiths: https://rapseygriffiths.com.au/tax-debt-on-credit-report-insolvency-newcastle-nsw/

Rapsey Griffiths. (2023). *5 situations where a company Director could be personally liable for its debts.* Retrieved from Rapsey Griffiths: https://rapseygriffiths.com.au/director-liable-compadebts-insolvency-newcastle-nsw/

Rapsey Griffiths. (2023). *6 Ways To Spot An Ineffective Management Team.* Retrieved from Rapsey Griffiths: https://rapseygriffiths.com.au/6-ways-to-spot-an-ineffective-management-team/

Rapsey Griffiths. (2023). *7 strategies for turnaround - Leadership cuts and reshuffling (Part 2 of 7).* Retrieved from Rapsey Griffiths: https://rapseygriffiths.com.au/7-strategies-for-turnaround-crisis-stabilisation-part-2-of-7/

Rapsey Griffiths. (2023). *7 strategies of turnaround.* Retrieved from Rapsey Griffiths: https://rapseygriffiths.com.au/strategies-of-turnaround/

Rapsey Griffiths. (2023). *7 strategies of turnaround - Crisis stabilisation (Part 1 of 7).* Retrieved from Rapsey Griffiths: https://rapseygriffiths.com.au/7-strategies-for-turnaround-crisis-stabilisation-part-1-of-7/

Rapsey Griffiths. (2023). *8 ways to minimise cash flow problems in your business.* Retrieved from Rapsey Griffiths: https://rapseygriffiths.com.au/cash-flow-problems-business-insolvency-newcastle-nsw/

Rapsey Griffiths. (2023). *A Creditor's rights - The new rules of Liquidation.* Retrieved from Rapsey Griffiths: https://rapseygriffiths.com.au/creditor-clients-customer-going-into-liquidation-and-what-to-do/

Rapsey Griffiths. (2023). *Accountants and insolvent clients: 3 ways to avoid unfair preference claims.* Retrieved from Rapsey Griffiths: https://rapseygriffiths.com.au/unfair-preference-claim-insolvency-newcastle-nsw/

Rapsey Griffiths. (2023). *Accountants: How to stop your clients getting burnt by illegal phoenix activity.* Retrieved from Rapsey Griffiths: https://rapseygriffiths.com.au/accountants-how-to-stop-your-clients-getting-burnt-by-illegal-phoenix-activity/

Rapsey Griffiths. (2023). *An accountant's guide to advising clients on Safe Harbour.* Retrieved from Rapsey Griffiths: https://rapseygriffiths.com.au/the-accountants-guide-to-advising-clients-on-safe-harbour/

Rapsey Griffiths. (2023). *Are Trust Assets as Safe as You Think? Corporate Trustees and Liquidation.* Retrieved from Rapsey Griffiths: https://rapseygriffiths.com.au/are-trust-assets-as-safe-as-you-think-corporate-trustees-and-liquidation/

Rapsey Griffiths. (2023). *Asset protection structure for SME owners that loan money to their business.* Retrieved from Rapsey Griffiths: https://rapseygriffiths.com.au/asset-protection-structure-for-sme-owners-that-loan-money-to-their-business/

Rapsey Griffiths. (2023). *Assets acquired after bankruptcy: What will happen to yours?* Retrieved from Rapsey Griffiths: https://rapseygriffiths.com.au/acquired-assets-bankruptcy-insolvency-newcastle-nsw/

Rapsey Griffiths. (2023). *Assets, debts & income in bankruptcy.* Retrieved from Rapsey Griffiths: https://rapseygriffiths.com.au/tools-and-resources/information-advice/bankruptcy-and-personal-insolvency/assets-debts-and-income-in-bankruptcy/

Rapsey Griffiths. (2023). *ATO Debt: How to get your debt arrangement accepted.* Retrieved from Rapsey Griffiths: https://rapseygriffiths.com.au/ato-debt-agreement-insolvency-newcastle-nsw/

Rapsey Griffiths. (2023). *Banking on it: 7 tips to help businesses deal with a bank during a financial crisis.* Retrieved from Rapsey Griffiths: https://rapseygriffiths.com.au/banking-on-it-7-tips-to-help-businesses-deal-with-a-bank-during-a-financial-crisis/

Rapsey Griffiths. (2023). *Bankruptcy & discretionary trusts.* Retrieved from Rapsey Griffiths: https://rapseygriffiths.com.au/tools-and-resources/information-advice/bankruptcy-and-personal-insolvency/bankruptcy-and-discretionary-trusts/

Rapsey Griffiths. (2023). *Bankruptcy & employment.* Retrieved from Rapsey Griffiths: https://rapseygriffiths.com.au/tools-and-resources/information-advice/bankruptcy-and-personal-insolvency/bankruptcy-and-employment/

Rapsey Griffiths. (2023). *Bankruptcy & houses.* Retrieved from Rapsey Griffiths: https://rapseygriffiths.com.au/tools-and-resources/information-advice/bankruptcy-and-personal-insolvency/bankruptcy-and-house/

Rapsey Griffiths. (2023). *Bankruptcy & personal insolvency.* Retrieved from Rapsey Griffiths: https://rapseygriffiths.com.au/tools-and-resources/information-advice/bankruptcy-and-personal-insolvency/

Rapsey Griffiths. (2023). *Business in trouble? 3 options to consider if your company is facing financial hardship.* Retrieved from Rapsey Griffiths: https://rapseygriffiths.com.au/fnancial-hardship-in-business-insolvency-newcastle-nsw/

Rapsey Griffiths. (2023). *Business turnaround – the questions you need to ask yourself to survive.* Retrieved from Rapsey Griffiths: https://rapseygriffiths.com.au/business-turnaround-questions-need-ask-survive/

Rapsey Griffiths. (2023). *Cancellation or annulment of bankruptcy.* Retrieved from Rapsey Griffiths: https://rapseygriffiths.com.au/tools-and-resources/information-advice/bankruptcy-and-personal-insolvency/cancellation-or-annulment-of-bankruptcy/

Rapsey Griffiths. (2023). *Cash flow problems: the whats, whys and hows of survival.* Retrieved from Rapsey Griffiths: https://rapseygriffiths.com.au/cash-flow-problems-the-whats-whys-and-hows-of-survival/

Rapsey Griffiths. (2023). *Christmas Crisis? 7 Tips For Avoiding The Christmas Cashflow Crunch.* Retrieved from Rapsey Griffiths: https://rapseygriffiths.com.au/christmas-crisis-7-tips-for-avoiding-the-christmas-cashflow-crunch/

Rapsey Griffiths. (2023). *Communicate to re-accumulate: why talking is key to successful business turnaround.* Retrieved from Rapsey Griffiths: https://rapseygriffiths.com.au/communicate-to-re-accumulate-why-talking-is-key-to-successful-business-turnaround/

Rapsey Griffiths. (2023). *COVID-19: How to Manage Your SME Cash Flow During a Crisis.* Retrieved from Rapsey Griffiths: https://rapseygriffiths.com.au/covid-19-how-to-manage-your-sme-cash-flow-during-a-crisis/

Rapsey Griffiths. (2023). *Discharge & finalisation of bankruptcy.* Retrieved from Rapsey Griffiths: https://rapseygriffiths.com.au/tools-and-resources/information-advice/bankruptcy-and-personal-insolvency/discharge-and-finalisation-of-bankruptcy/

Rapsey Griffiths. (2023). *Grounded or Unfounded?: Can You Travel Overseas If You're Bankrupt?* Retrieved from Rapsey Griffiths: https://rapseygriffiths.com.au/grounded-or-unfounded-can-you-travel-overseas-if-youre-bankrupt/

Rapsey Griffiths. (2023). *How the Bankruptcy Act can help you deal with a deceased's estate when they are insolvent.* Retrieved from Rapsey Griffiths: https://rapseygriffiths.com.au/insolvent-deceased-estates-insolvency-newcastle-nsw/

Rapsey Griffiths. (2023). *Insolvency inquiry told businesses 'not willing to ask for help'.* Retrieved from Rapsey Griffiths: https://rapseygriffiths.com.au/insolvency-inquiry-told-businesses-not-willing-to-ask-for-help/

Rapsey Griffiths. (2023). *Insolvent trading safe harbour: What does it mean for business turnaround strategy?* Retrieved from Rapsey Griffiths: https://rapseygriffiths.com.au/insolvent-trading-safe-harbour-business-turnaround/

Rapsey Griffiths. (2023). *It's not the economy, stupid: 6 small business management mistakes to stop making.* Retrieved from Rapsey Griffiths: https://rapseygriffiths.com.au/business-management-mistakes-insolvency-newcastle-nsw/

Rapsey Griffiths. (2023). *Licensed to Earn: 7 Cases Where Bankruptcy Can Affect Your Employment.* Retrieved from Rapsey Griffiths: https://rapseygriffiths.com.au/licensed-to-earn-7-cases-where-bankruptcy-can-affect-your-employment/

Rapsey Griffiths. (2023). *Liquidator cometh: Your client receives a demand for an unfair preference. Now what?* Retrieved from Rapsey Griffiths: https://rapseygriffiths.com.au/the-liquidator-cometh-your-client-receives-a-demand-for-an-unfair-preference-now-what/

Rapsey Griffiths. (2023). *Making costly mistakes? 6 ways to reduce business costs and increase your profits.* Retrieved from Rapsey Griffiths: https://rapseygriffiths.com.au/reduce-business-costs-insolvency-newcastle-nsw/

Rapsey Griffiths. (2023). *Paying it back – how going bankrupt will affect your income.* Retrieved from Rapsey Griffiths: https://rapseygriffiths.com.au/understanding-bankruptcy-income-contributions-newcastle-nsw/

Rapsey Griffiths. (2023). *Personal insolvency & legal advice.* Retrieved from Rapsey Griffiths: https://rapseygriffiths.com.au/tools-and-resources/information-advice/bankruptcy-and-personal-insolvency/personal-insolvency-and-legal-advice/

Rapsey Griffiths. (2023). *Saving a business in trouble: The 4 stages of awareness.* Retrieved from Rapsey Griffiths: https://rapseygriffiths.com.au/saving-business-in-trouble-insolvency-newcastle-nsw/

Rapsey Griffiths. (2023). *Signs of strife: Is bankruptcy the right option for a client?* Retrieved from Rapsey Griffiths: https://rapseygriffiths.com.au/signs-of-strife-is-bankruptcy-the-right-option-for-a-client/

Rapsey Griffiths. (2023). *Six steps to a successful business turnaround: Client case study.* Retrieved from Rapsey Griffiths: https://rapseygriffiths.com.au/successful-business-financial-difficulty-turnaround/

Rapsey Griffiths. (2023). *Staying solvent in Australia's building and construction industry.* Retrieved from Rapsey Griffiths: https://rapseygriffiths.com.au/insolvency-in-building-and-construction-industry/

Rapsey Griffiths. (2023). *Tax refunds during bankruptcy.* Retrieved from Rapsey Griffiths: https://rapseygriffiths.com.au/tools-and-resources/information-advice/bankruptcy-and-personal-insolvency/tax-refunds-during-bankruptcy/

Rapsey Griffiths. (2023). *The 6 stages of debt, and whether to declare bankruptcy.* Retrieved from Rapsey Griffiths: https://rapseygriffiths.com.au/declaring-bankruptcy-insolvency-newcastle-nsw/

Rapsey Griffiths. (2023). *The benefits of Members' Voluntary Liquidation.* Retrieved from Rapsey Griffiths: https://rapseygriffiths.com.au/what-is-a-members-voluntary-liquidation-and-how-is-it-arranged/

Rapsey Griffiths. (2023). *The rights of landlords and liquidators when a tenant is insolvent.* Retrieved from Rapsey Griffiths: https://rapseygriffiths.com.au/landlord-liquidator-tenant-insolvency-newcastle/

Rapsey Griffiths. (2023). *Turnaround engagement: 3 steps to help your business survive.* Retrieved from Rapsey Griffiths: https://rapseygriffiths.com.au/turnaround-engagements-insolvency-newcastle-nsw/

Rapsey Griffiths. (2023). *Update: Director Penalty Notice (DPN) regime extended to include GST liabilities.* Retrieved from Rapsey Griffiths: https://rapseygriffiths.com.au/update-director-penalty-notice-dpn-regime-extended-to-include-gst-liabilities/

Rapsey Griffiths. (2023). *Warning signs your client's business could be in trouble.* Retrieved from Rapsey Griffiths: https://rapseygriffiths.com.au/warning-signs-your-clients-business-could-be-in-trouble/

Rapsey Griffiths. (2023). *What happens to your assets when you file for bankruptcy.* Retrieved from Rapsey Griffiths: https://rapseygriffiths.com.au/declaring-bankruptcy-assets-insolvency-newcastle-nsw/

Rapsey Griffiths. (2023). *What is a chief restructuring officer – and could one save your business?* Retrieved from Rapsey Griffiths: https://rapseygriffiths.com.au/what-is-a-chief-restructuring-officer/

Rapsey Griffiths. (2023). *When liquidation becomes personal.* Retrieved from Rapsey Griffiths: https://rapseygriffiths.com.au/client-company-going-into-liquidation-determining-personal-liabilities/

Rapsey Griffiths. (2023). *When to call in a turnaround expert to help a client in financial strife.* Retrieved from Rapsey Griffiths: https://rapseygriffiths.com.au/when-to-call-in-a-turnaround-expert-to-help-a-client-in-financial-strife/

Rapsey Griffiths. (2023). *Why your clients must act quickly if they receive a Statutory Demand.* Retrieved from https://rapseygriffiths.com.au/statutory-demand-creditor-insolvency-newcastle-nsw/

Rapsey Griffiths. (2023). *Winding up a solvent company? The Pro's and Con's of Member's Voluntary Liquidation (MVL) vs Deregistration.* Retrieved from Rapsey Griffiths: https://rapseygriffiths.com.au/members-voluntary-liquidation-solvent-company/

Rapsey Griffiths. (2023). *Zero-based budgeting: Cutting costs by starting financially from scratch.* Retrieved from Rapsey Griffiths: https://rapseygriffiths.com.au/zero-based-budgeting-cutting-costs-by-starting-financially-from-scratch/

Richardson, B., Nwankwo, S., & Richardson, S. (1944). Understanding the Causes of Business Failure Crises: Generic Failure Types: Boiled Frogs, Drowned Frogs, Bullfrogs and Tadpoles. *Management Decisions, 32*(4), 9-22.

Robba, J. (2018, May 24). *Lockdown DPNs and personal liability.* Retrieved from Worrells: https://worrells.net.au/resources/news/lockdown-dpns-and-personal-liability

Robson Cotter Insolvency Group. (2022, December 14). *Small Business Restructuring – How is the process going...?* Retrieved from https://www.rcinsol.com.au/blog/ small-business-restructuring-how-are-they-going/

Robson Cotter Insolvency Group. (2022, December 14). *Small Business Restructuring – How is the process going...?* Retrieved from https://www.rcinsol.com.au/blog/small-business-restructuring-how-are-they-going/

Sanderson, C. (2018, September 18). *Voluntary Administrations – don't get too excited about the chances of success.* Retrieved from Dissolve: https://www.dissolve.com.au/blog/ voluntary-administrations-dont-get-too-excited-about-the-chances-of-success/

Sanlam. (2023). *Financial Solutions for Business Owners: Business Turnaround Book.* Retrieved June 2023

Sarakbi, Y. (2022, July 29). *Poor tax compliance history and its effects on a company's ability to restructure.* Retrieved from Worrells: https://worrells.net.au/resources/news/ poor-tax-compliance-history-and-its-effects-on-a-company-s-ability-to-restructure

Sewell & Kettle. (2012, November 20). *What is an AllPAAP and how can security agreements protect you from non-payment?* Retrieved from Sewell & Kettle: https://sklaw.au/blog/ fixed-and-floating-charges-the-royal-flush/

Sewell & Kettle. (2018, September 25). *Applications to wind up a company in insolvency.* Retrieved from Sewell & Kettle: https://sklawyers.com.au/blog/winding-up-application/

Sewell & Kettle. (2018, October 21). *What are the grounds to set-aside a statutory demand?* Retrieved from Sewell & Kettle: https://sklawyers.com.au/blog/set-aside-a-statutory-demand/

Sewell & Kettle. (2018, September 27). *What is the difference between a deed and an agreement?* Retrieved from Sewell & Kettle: https://sklawyers.com.au/blog/deed/

Sewell & Kettle. (2019, June 7). *How do you respond to an ATO garnishee notice?* Retrieved from Sewell & Kettle: https://sklawyers.com.au/blog/respond-ato-garnishee-notice/

Sewell & Kettle. (2019, November 1). *How to negotiate an ATO payment plan (small businesses).* Retrieved from Sewell & Kettle: https://sklawyers.com.au/blog/negotiate-ato-payment-plan/

Sewell & Kettle. (2019, July 17). *What are the new penalties for directors?* Retrieved from Sewell & Kettle: https://sklawyers.com.au/blog/new-penalties-for-directors/

Sewell & Kettle. (2020, June 12). *How does a liquidator decide whether to commence an insolvent trading claim?* Retrieved from Sewell & Kettle: https://sklawyers.com.au/blog/ liquidator-commence-insolvent-trading-claim/

Sewell & Kettle. (2020, May 15). *How to avoid a voluntary administration of your company (for small or medium-sized enterprises).* Retrieved from Sewell & Kettle: https://sklawyers.com. au/blog/avoid-voluntary-administration/

Sewell & Kettle. (2020, November 12). *Insolvent Trading: Complete Explanation for SMEs.* Retrieved from Sewell & Kettle: https://sklaw.au/blog/insolvent- trading/

Sewell & Kettle. (2020, September 2). *Offshore Tax Havens: A Guide for Australian Investors.* Retrieved from Sewell & Kettle: https://sklaw.au/blog/offshore-tax-havens/

Sewell & Kettle. (2020, September 3). *The Complete Guide to Illegal Phoenix Activity.* Retrieved from Sewell & Kettle: https://sklawyers.com.au/blog/phoenix-activity/

Sewell & Kettle. (2020, October 19). *The Complete Guide to Trading Trusts for small and medium-sized business.* Retrieved from Sewell & Kettle: https://sklawyers.com.au/blog/trading-trust/

Sewell & Kettle. (2020, July 23). *The Complete Guide to Voluntary Administration.* Retrieved from Sewell & Kettle: https://sklawyers.com.au/blog/voluntary-administration/

Sewell & Kettle. (2020, December 21). *The Ultimate Guide to Liquidation Part 2: Preparing for Liquidation.* Retrieved from Sewell & Kettle: https://sklawyers.com.au/blog/preparing-for-liquidation/

Sewell & Kettle. (2020, December 18). *Ultimate Guide to Liquidation Part 1: What is Liquidation?* Retrieved from Sewell & Kettle: https://sklawyers.com.au/blog/what-is-liquidation/

Sewell & Kettle. (2020, December 21). *Ultimate Guide to Liquidation Part 3: Responding to liquidation.* Retrieved from Sewell & Kettle: https://sklawyers.com.au/blog/responding-to-liquidation/

Sewell & Kettle. (2020, April 30). *What is the role of solicitors in the restructuring of insolvent small or medium-sized businesses today?* Retrieved from Sewell & Kettle: https://sklawyers.com.au/blog/solicitor-role-restructuring/

Sewell & Kettle. (2020, March 6). *What needs to be changed in Australian insolvency law: More carrots and less stick for directors.* Retrieved from Sewell & Kettle: https://sklawyers.com.au/blog/what-is-the-purpose-of-our-insolvency-law-australia-needs-more-carrot-and-less-stick/

Sewell & Kettle. (2020, September 3). *What should a Pre-Insolvency Adviser (a lawyer, accountant or other professional) do to help a financially troubled small or medium-sized business?* Retrieved from Sewell & Kettle: https://sklawyers.com.au/blog/pre-insolvency-advisers/

Sewell & Kettle. (2020, July). *What you need to know before you pre-pack (to avoid phoenix activity).* Retrieved from Sewell & Kettle: https://sklaw.au/white-papers/pre-pack-insolvency-arrangement/

Sewell & Kettle. (2020, March 11). *When is a construction company insolvent?* Retrieved from Sewell & Kettle: https://sklaw.au/blog/when-construction-company-insolvent/

Sewell & Kettle. (2020, November 18). *Zombie Companies: Is your business walking dead? Complete Guide for SMEs.* Retrieved from Sewell & Kettle: https://sklawyers.com.au/blog/zombie-companies/

Sewell & Kettle. (2021, June 7). *A Complete Guide to the Small Business Restructuring Process.* Retrieved from Sewell & Kettle: https://sklaw.au/blog/a-complete-guide-to-simplified-debt-restructuring/

Sewell & Kettle. (2021, October 25). *Are Directors' Salaries 'Voidable Transactions' in a Winding Up?* Retrieved from Sewell & Kettle: https://sklawyers.com.au/blog/are-directors-salaries-voidable-transactions-in-winding-up/

Sewell & Kettle. (2021, August 5). *Business Survival Series: Is the problem an inside problem or an outside problem?* Retrieved from Sewell & Kettle: https://sklaw.au/blog/swot-inside-or-outside-problem/

Sewell & Kettle. (2021, April 29). *Business Survival Series: Many Turnaround Consultants Don't Want to Turn Your Business Around.* Retrieved from Sewell & Kettle: https://sklaw.au/blog/turnaround-consultants-dont-want-to-turn-your-business-around/

Sewell & Kettle. (2021, April 26). *Business Survival Series: Misconceptions About Starting a Business*. Retrieved from Sewell & Kettle: https://sklawyers.com.au/blog/misconceptions-about-starting-business/

Sewell & Kettle. (2021, June 16). *Business Survival Series: Pareto Principle*. Retrieved from Sewell & Kettle: https://sklaw.au/blog/business-survival-series-pareto-principle/

Sewell & Kettle. (2021, June 28). *Business Survival Series: Parts of a Business to Save*. Retrieved from Sewell & Kettle: https://sklaw.au/blog/business-survival-series-parts-business-to-save/

Sewell & Kettle. (2021, May 17). *Business Survival Series: Respect Your Creditors*. Retrieved from Sewell & Kettle: https://sklaw.au/blog/business-survival-series-respect-your-creditors/

Sewell & Kettle. (2021, August 10). *Business Survival Series: You're too limited by bounded rationality so get an independent assessment*. Retrieved from Sewell & Kettle: https://sklaw.au/blog/insolvent-get-independent-assessment/

Sewell & Kettle. (2021, October 29). *Can a Liquidator Ignore 'Retention of Title' Claims and Keep Inventory when a Business is put into Liquidation?* Retrieved from Sewell & Kettle: https://sklaw.au/blog/can-liquidator-ignore-retention-of-title-claims/

Sewell & Kettle. (2021, November 18). *How Can a Liquidator Recover 'Unfair Loans'?* Retrieved from Sewell & Kettle: https://sklawyers.com.au/blog/how-can-liquidator-recover-unfair-loans/

Sewell & Kettle. (2021, July 6). *How Can Liquidators Obtain a Warrant to Seize Company Property?* Retrieved from Sewell & Kettle: https://sklaw.au/blog/how-can-liquidators-obtain-warrant-to-seize-company-property/

Sewell & Kettle. (2021, September 22). *How Do You Work Out if a Liquidator Is Funded?* Retrieved from Sewell & Kettle: https://sklaw.au/blog/how-liquidator-is-funded/

Sewell & Kettle. (2021, November 11). *How Does the ATO Fund Liquidation Claims?* Retrieved from Sewell & Kettle: https://sklaw.au/blog/how-does-the-ato-fund-liquidation-claims/

Sewell & Kettle. (2021, November 25). *Insolvency practitioners in Australia are angry and frustrated. Why is that, and why is it important to know?* Retrieved from Sewell & Kettle: https://sklawyers.com.au/blog/insolvency-practitioners-in-australia-angry-and-frustrated/

Sewell & Kettle. (2021, August 5). *Is the problem an inside problem or an outside problem?* Retrieved from Sewell & Kettle: https://sklaw.au/blog/swot-inside-or-outside-problem/

Sewell & Kettle. (2021, September 30). *Selecting the right liquidator for an insolvent business*. Retrieved from Sewell & Kettle: https://sklaw.au/blog/selecting-right-liquidator-for-insolvent-business/

Sewell & Kettle. (2021, June 22). *The Status of a Trust when a Corporate Trustee goes into Liquidation?* Retrieved from Sewell & Kettle: https://sklaw.au/blog/what-is-the-status-of-trust-when-corporate-trustee-goes-into-liquidation/

Sewell & Kettle. (2021, May 31). *What are Unfair Preference Claims by a Company Liquidator?* Retrieved from Sewell & Kettle: https://sklaw.au/blog/what-are-unfair-preference-claims-by-company-liquidator/

Sewell & Kettle. (2021, August 19). *What is an Uncommercial Transaction?* Retrieved from Sewell & Kettle: https://sklaw.au/blog/what-is-an-uncommercial-transaction/

Sewell & Kettle. (2021, August 31). *What is an Unreasonable Director-Related Transaction?* Retrieved from Sewell & Kettle: https://sklaw.au/blog/what-is-unreasonable-director-related-transaction/

Sewell & Kettle. (2021, July 15). *What is the Running Account Defence to an Unfair Preference Claim?* Retrieved from Sewell & Kettle: https://sklaw.au/blog/running-account-defence-unfair-preference-claim/

Sewell & Kettle. (2021, October 15). *Who should be the architect of a turnaround?* Retrieved from Sewell & Kettle: https://sklawyers.com.au/blog/who-should-be-the-architect-of-a-turnaround/

Sewell & Kettle. (2022, February 5). *Business Survival Series: The Most Important Questions for a Business to Answer on Day 1 of a Turnaround.* Retrieved from Sewell & Kettle: https://sklaw.au/blog/most-important-questions-to-answer-turnaround/

Sewell & Kettle. (2022, June 28). *If Economic Distress, Liquidate. If Financial Distress, Save through Restructure.* Retrieved from Sewell & Kettle: https://sklaw.au/blog/if-economic-distress-liquidate-if-financial-distress-save-through-restructure/

Sewell & Kettle. (2022, August 31). *Regular cash flow projections and comparison to actuals.* Retrieved from Sewell & Kettle: https://sklaw.au/blog/regular-cash-flow-projections-and-comparison-to-actuals/

Sewell & Kettle. (2022, May 23). *The Complete Guide to working out whether your troubled business should go into Voluntary Administration, Small Business Restructuring or just be liquidated?* Retrieved from Sewell & Kettle: https://sklaw.au/blog/complete-guide-to-working-out-whether-your-troubled-business-should-go-into-va-sbr-or-liquidation/

Sewell & Kettle. (2022, August 11). *What are the good parts of the Australian voluntary administration process?* Retrieved from Sewell & Kettle: https://sklaw.au/blog/what-are-good-parts-of-australian-va-process/

Sewell & Kettle. (2023). *Cash-flow test.* Retrieved from Sewell & Kettle: https://sklaw.au/dictionary/cash-flow-test/

Sewell & Kettle. (2023). *Statement of Claim.* Retrieved from Sewell & Kettle: https://sklaw.au/clients/types-legal-process/statement-claim/

Sewell & Kettle. (2023, March 20). *Why a financially troubled business should create a three factor budget.* Retrieved from Sewell & Kettle: https://sklaw.au/blog/why-a-financially-troubled-business-should-create-a-three-factor-budget/

Sewell, B. (2020, July 22). *Avoiding The Wall When Trouble Looms.* Retrieved from ATN Australian Transport News: https://www.fullyloaded.com.au/industry-news/2007/opinion-avoiding-the-wall

Shahzaib. (2023, May 5). *Scott Dylan's Tips for Managing Stakeholder Expectations in Business Turnaround.* Retrieved from Newsbreak: https://original.newsbreak.com/@shahzaib-1620246/3014361309750-scott-dylan-s-tips-for-managing-stakeholder-expectations-in-business-turnaround

Shaw, A. A. (2023). *Turnaround Strategy – Definition, Types, Stages & Examples.* Retrieved from Marketing Tutor: https://marketingtutor.net/turnaround-strategy/

Shukla, T. (2017, July 10). *SpiceJet's fairytale turnaround to become world's best aviation stock.* Retrieved from Mint: https://www.livemint.com/Companies/T2BOBSwziSYSnEDPMJ2xEM/The-SpiceJet-turnaround-story-and-how-it-became-worlds-best.html

Siu, A. (2022, July 28). *Alternate use of the voluntary administration moratorium.* Retrieved from Worrells: https://worrells.net.au/resources/news/alternate-use-of-the-voluntary-administration-moratorium

Skae, O. (2018, February 5). *Steinhoff – the drowned frog.* Retrieved from Critical Thought: https://www.ru.ac.za/criticalthought/newssliderfeed3/steinhoffthedrownedfrog.html

Slatter, S., & Lovett, D. (1999). *Corporate Turnaround - Managing Companies in Distress.* Penguin.

Soni, T. (2015). *Zero-based budgeting.* Retrieved from Deloitte: https://www.deloitte.com/global/en/services/consulting/perspectives/gx-zero-based-budgeting.html

Spacey, J. (2020, April 5). *9 Examples of Turnaround Management.* Retrieved from Simplicable: https://simplicable.com/en/turnaround-management

Sprekos, P. (2022, December 13). *4 Essential Money Management Tips for First Time Business Owners.* Retrieved from LinkedIn: https://www.linkedin.com/pulse/4-essential-money-management-tips-first-time-business-peter-sprekos/?trackingId=eUbU6vHGRFmc4QUx%2FBgCEw%3D%3D

SV Partners. (2022). *Simplified Liquidation Process.* Retrieved from https://svpartners.com.au/services/solutions-for-businesses/simplified-liquidation/

SV Partners. (2022). *Small Business Restructure Process.* Retrieved from https://svpartners.com.au/services/solutions-for-businesses/small-business-restructure-process/

The Balanced Kiwi. (2023). *The Boiled Frog: A cautionary tale.* Retrieved from The Balanced Kiwi: https://thebalancedkiwi.com/the-boiled-frog/

The Editors of Encylopedia Britannica. (2023, May 5). *Conrad Black.* Retrieved from Britannica: https://www.britannica.com/biography/Conrad-Black

The Strategy Story. (2023). *Turnaround Strategies: Explained with examples and case study.* Retrieved from The Strategy Story: https://thestrategystory.com/blog/turnaround-strategies-explained-with-examples-and-case-study/

Thomas, G. (2019, September 14). *The Ansett Collapse.* Retrieved from Australian Aviation: https://australianaviation.com.au/2019/09/from-the-archives-the-ansett-collapse/

Tikici, M., Omay, E., Derin, N., Nur Seckin, S., & Cureoglu, M. (2011). Operating turnaround strategies during crisis periods: Seyda Nur Seckin; Mehmet Cureoglu. *Procedia Social and Behavioral Sciences. 24,* pp. 49–60. Elsevier Ltd. doi:10.1016/J.SBSPRO.2011.09.046

UK Administrators. (2023, May). *The decline and recovery curve of business rescue.* Retrieved from https://www.ukadministrators.org.uk/7-steps-business-turnaround/

Vantage Performance. (2023). *Common Mistakes of Bad Management.* Retrieved from https://www.vantageperformance.com.au/common-mistakes-of-bad-management/

Vorbach, P., & Pan, K. (2017, December). Leading the Corporate Turnaround. *Australian Restructuring Insolvency & Turnaround Journal,* 10-15.

Wachman, R. (2007, June 25). *How competition ate away Britain's chemicals giant.* Retrieved from The Guardian: https://www.theguardian.com/business/2007/jun/24/theobserver.observerbusiness5

Ward, A. (2020, June 30). *Using a section 73 proposal to annul a bankruptcy.* Retrieved from Worrells: https://worrells.net.au/resources/news/using-a-section-73-proposal-to-annul-a-bankruptcy?utm_source=Mondaq&utm_medium=syndication&utm_campaign=LinkedIn-integration

Waterstone Insolvency. (2023). *Part XIV Compromise.* Retrieved from Waterstone Insolvency: https://waterstone.co.nz/services/part-xiv-compromise/

Webber, & Weller. (2002). *The post-retrenchment labour market experiences of Ansett workers.* School of Anthropology, Geography and Environmental Studies, University of Melbourne.

Whitney, J. O. (1987, Septemeber). *Turnaround Management Every Day.* Retrieved from Harvard Business Review: https://hbr.org/1987/09/turnaround-management-every-day

Whittle, N. (2022, June 22). *Australia/New Zealand insolvency law comparison.* Retrieved from Chapman Tripp: https://chapmantripp.com/trends-insights/rescue-recovery-2022/australian-new-zealand-insolvency-law-comparison/

Wikipedia. (2023). *Ansett Australia.* Retrieved from https://en.wikipedia.org/wiki/Ansett_Australia#:~:text=Despite%20public%20pleas%2C%20the%20Australian,into%20voluntary%20administration%20with%20PriceWaterhouseCoopers.

Wikipedia. (2023). *Clive Sinclair.* Retrieved from Wikipedia: https://en.wikipedia.org/wiki/Clive_Sinclair

Wikipedia. (2023). *Lord of the Flies.* Retrieved from Wikipedia: https://en.wikipedia.org/wiki/Lord_of_the_Flies

Wikipedia. (2023). *Polymath.* Retrieved from Wikipedia: https://en.wikipedia.org/wiki/Polymath

Wikipedia. (2023). *Rolodex.* Retrieved from Wikipedia: https://en.wikipedia.org/wiki/Rolodex#:~:text=A%20Rolodex%20is%20a%20rotating,to%20store%20business%20contact%20information.

Wikipedia. (2023, May). *Triage.* Retrieved from Wikipedia: https:en.wikipedia.org/wiki/triage

Wikipedia. (2023). *Turnaround management.* Retrieved from Wikipedia: https://en.wikipedia.org/wiki/Turnaround_management

Wilmot, B. (2023, May 4). *Mahercorp founder working on turnaround plan.* Retrieved from Herald Sun: https://www.heraldsun.com.au/business/mahercorp-founder-working-on-turnaround-plan/news-story/a1ea9c7e8daeof5f606ff4cf7b03bcf0

Withane, T. (2022, July 01). *Take a strategic approach to dealing with DPNs.* Retrieved from Accountants Daily: https://www.accountantsdaily.com.au/business/17233-a-strategic-approach-to-dealing-with-dpns

Worrells. (2022/23). Guide to Corporate Insolvency.

Worrells. (2007, February 1). *What makes a good Section 73 Proposal?* Retrieved from Worrells: https://worrells.net.au/resources/news/what-makes-a-good-section-73-proposal

Worrells. (2023, May 1). *What are personal insolvency agreements and how can they help?* Retrieved from https://worrells.net.au/resources/news/what-are-personal-insolvency-agreements-and-how-can-they-help

Worrells Solvency & Forensic Accountants. (2021/22). Guide to Personal Insolvency. *A Fresh Start.*

Xero. (2023). *Money matters: Navigating the impact of economic conditions on the cash flow of New Zealand small businesses.* Wellington: Xero New Zealand.